D1527565

BEGINNING THE SEARCH

A Young Adults'
Approach to *A Search
for God*

by
Shirley G. Clement and
Virginia Fields

A.R.E. PRESS • VIRGINIA BEACH • VIRGINIA

Dedication

With praise to God and thanks to our families and study groups, we dedicate this book to the Christ who lives in everyone.

Printed in the U.S.A.

CONTENTS

PREFACE

Beginning the Search is based on *A Search for God,* Book I, written by members of an A.R.E. Study Group who asked the "sleeping" Edgar Cayce questions concerning the spiritual laws of life. The principles he gave in his readings were not new, for the search for God is as old as mankind. However, the emphasis of the readings was on *applying* spiritual concepts in daily life, rather than just gathering information about them.

Beginning the Search was written to acquaint beginning searchers with the concepts of the original book. The authors have included charts, games, puzzles, and other activities which can help individual readers, as well as study groups, understand and apply the book's lessons.

Use of many modern translations makes the Bible quotations easy to read, and it can help searchers become aware that truth may be expressed in many ways. Abbreviations for the various Bibles quoted are as follows: *King James Version,* KJV; *Jerusalem Bible,* JB; *New Testament* (Lamsa), LV; *Living Bible,* LB; *New Catholic Edition,* NCE; *New English Bible,* NEB; *New Testament in Modern English* (Phillips), PB; *Revised Standard Version,* RSV; *The Torah, Torah.*

Hints for Using *Beginning the Search*

Each chapter has a prayer affirmation designed to help the searcher live the chapter's lesson. The affirmation needs to be included in the searcher's daily prayer and meditation periods.

The study group activities included at the end of each lesson are suggestions designed to enhance group participation and help searchers live the truths. Material in each chapter should require more than one meeting for reading and discussion, so several activities have been included with each lesson. Allow fifteen to thirty minutes for the activities at the end of each meeting. Group members should save their poetry, handwork, etc., throughout the lessons to complete an activity at the end of Lesson 12. Individuals not in study groups may enrich their studies with the "Individual Growth Experiences" also included with the lessons.

The Handbook for A.R.E. Study Groups, published by the A.R.E. Press, is a "must" for group work. It gives valuable information on how to organize a group and apply the lessons in each chapter. Another helpful book for study groups is *Edgar Cayce and Group Dynamics,* by Worth Kidd, also from the A.R.E. Press.

Virginia Fields
Shirley G. Clement

MEDITATION

Bible Verse: "Be still, and know that I am God. . ."
(Psalms 46:10, KJV)

Prayer Affirmation: The Lord's Prayer

> "Our Father which art in heaven,
> Hallowed be Thy name.
> Thy kingdom come. Thy will be done in earth,
>   as it is in heaven.
> Give us this day our daily bread.
> And forgive us our debts,
>   as we forgive our debtors.
> And lead us not into temptation, but deliver
>   us from evil:
> For Thine is the kingdom, and the power,
>   and the glory, for ever. Amen."
> (Matthew 6:9-13, KJV)

Introduction

Many of us want to find the answers to life's biggest questions: Why were we born? Does life have a purpose? What is death? Is there life after death? Does God really exist? If He does, who or what is He?[1] Can we communicate with Him? Until these questions are answered to our satisfaction, most of us feel an inner hunger that we try to satisfy. Some of us try to satisfy this longing through food, alcohol, or drug experiences. Others think that sex will fulfill these inner yearnings. Still others, thinking that "having fun" will answer all needs, constantly seek new pleasures. The desires and longings take various forms in different people's lives.

---

1. God is spirit (John 4:24), and so is neither male nor female. However, the authors have followed the Judeo-Christian tradition of referring to God in the masculine gender.

1

After trying various unfulfilling experiences, we eventually discover that we still feel incomplete and discontented. Finally we realize that the answers to life's questions are found not outside us, but within, and we begin to search for the Spiritual Essence of life—God. Once we find Him, we realize peace and contentment; we have the joy we were created to experience.

God is in continuous communication with man and constantly pours out His love to all. If we don't know Him, it is because we have blocked Him out through selfish thoughts and actions. To find Him, we need to begin to leave our selfishness behind us and commune with Him through prayer and meditation.

What Is Prayer?

What is prayer? Prayer is talking to God. As we pray, we need to empty ourselves of negative emotions that could keep us from knowing Him—worry, hatred, guilt, envy, resentment, fear, etc. We get our egos, our pride, out of the way so that we can receive God's guidance and help.

One of the surest blocks to effective prayer is self-righteousness. Jesus gave an example of this type of prayer. (See Luke 18:9-14, JB.)

> "He spoke the following parable to some people who prided themselves on being virtuous and despised everyone else, 'Two men went up to the Temple to pray, one a Pharisee, the other a tax collector. The Pharisee stood there and said this prayer to himself, "I thank you, God, that I am not grasping, unjust, adulterous like the rest of mankind, and particularly that I am not like this tax collector here. I fast twice a week; I pay tithes on all I get." ' "

Jesus contrasted the self-centered, self-righteous prayer of the Pharisee with the humility of the tax collector, who prayed, "God, be merciful to me, a sinner." Then Jesus said, ". . .everyone who exalts himself will be humbled, but the man who humbles himself will be exalted."

Jesus gave an example of the way to pray, commonly called "The Lord's Prayer" (printed as the prayer affirmation for this chapter). This perfect prayer can be used as a pattern for our own prayers.

What Is Meditation?

When we pray we *talk* to God; when we meditate we *listen* for His answer. Meditation is not daydreaming; it is stilling our

2

minds and our senses, so we can attune to the Divine within. At the height of meditation, we meet God and He communes with us. This is the real purpose of meditation.

Meditation is something no one else can do for us. (See Deuteronomy 30:11-14.) It is the way that we can reach beyond our senses, open the door to our own higher consciousness, meet God within, receive His guidance, and let Him express more fully in our lives. Meditation increases our understanding of ourselves, our kinship with God, and our relationship to others.

Can Prayer Take the Place of Meditation?

Both prayer and meditation are important, for one completes the other. Prayer prepares us for meditation by turning the conscious mind toward God, but prayer cannot take the place of meditation. We need to listen to God as well as to speak to Him. Also, meditation, communion with Him, is the basis for our mental and physical strength. Jesus said that He had nourishment, energy ("meat") no one knew about. He was referring to the strength received through His at-one-ment with God in the silence of meditation (John 4:32 and Cayce reading 281-13).

What Happens When We Pray and Meditate?

To understand the transforming power of prayer and meditation, we need to know something about the principles of vibration or motion. All matter is the result of one vibrating spiritual force—the spirit of life itself, God. Although this force is One, it vibrates at varying rates, which we perceive through our limited senses as different creations: sun, moon, stars, earth, minerals, plants, animals, people, etc. Our senses allow us to perceive only a small portion of the myriad expressions of God.

To help us understand how one force can appear as different creations, we can use water as an earthly example of this principle. Water, steam, ice, and snow are the same substance, but to the senses they appear to be different because of their different vibratory rates. In the same way, all of God's expressions, which seem to be different, are really made up of His one force vibrating at varying rates.

Each of us is a spiritual being made in God's image (Genesis 1:26). He gave us the power to co-create with Him. We create by varying the vibrations of our thoughts. We can use our thoughts to create in harmony with God's divine plan, or we can choose to express selfish, discordant creations. Our thoughts are important

3

because they affect the vibrations of the cosmos, the universe, the earth, other people, and ourselves.

Our thoughts affect our physical bodies, too. Our bodies are vibrations within the wholeness of the one force, with individual parts vibrating at varying rates. The nerves vibrate more rapidly than the dense bones, and the muscles have a lower frequency than the membranes, etc. The separately vibrating parts, all combined, produce the total vibratory rate of our individual bodies. This rate changes constantly, for it is affected by our dietary habits, our emotions, our thoughts, and our actions. The vibratory rate we create within ourselves brings about a state of well-being or varying degrees of disease. We are "at ease" when we are working in harmony with God and His law of love. We have mental, physical, or emotional "dis-ease" or distress when we live selfishly, putting us out of harmony with God's divine plan.

When we begin to pray and meditate, we can release powerful vibrations which make our thoughts and actions manifest more quickly. This can create problems for us if we do not let go of our selfish thought patterns. On the other hand, prayer and meditation can create great blessings for us as we let go of our self-centeredness and begin to work in loving harmony with others and with God. Our bodies become more spiritualized and healthy. Our minds grow more creative; new talents can bloom. We can become aware of the realms, the vibrations, beyond the limitations of our senses. We have a closer spiritual communion with God.

Before we begin to pray and meditate, we need to know more about ourselves, so that we can understand how God's life force works through us, how we can work in harmony with it, and how it can renew us physically, mentally, and spiritually.

Understanding the Body, Mind, and Spirit

Each of us is a soul composed of will, mind, and spirit, reflected in the earth as a body, mind, and spirit. These three parts of us must work in harmony for us to realize at-one-ment with God during meditation.

Understanding the Physical Body

Each of us is a universe in miniature. Just as God dwells in the outer universe, He is present in the physical body. In fact, the body is the temple, the place where we meet God (I Corinthians 3:16; 15:44).

God's creative force flows through wheels of vibrational energy, or *chakras*, in the soul body, and manifests through the seven ductless glands in the physical body. The glands of our endocrine system are the gonads (sex glands), Leydig (also called lyden), adrenals, thymus, thyroid, pineal and pituitary. We need to take care of our bodies and keep them balanced so God's energy can flow smoothly through us, keeping us in close communion with Him. Poor eating habits, lack of exercise, misuse of alcohol or drugs, or even physical injuries can inhibit this spiritual energy flow. If we have negative thoughts (anger, fear, resentment, etc.), we can temporarily prevent the energy from moving harmoniously through the glandular centers. Long-standing negative thinking habits can so inhibit the energy flow throughout the glandular system that disease is created. Anything that hinders the stream of God's spiritual energy through our bodies limits our ability to communicate with Him.

Let's examine a way that our thoughts can affect our bodies. Within the gonad center is the energy force known as *kundalini* or "serpent fire"—a strong creative energy. This force is kept in check from overpowering any unbalanced centers through the "control valve" of the Leydig. The Leydig keeps the kundalini force vibrating at a safe level until we are able to utilize it properly through spiritual development, when it becomes an energy field of great blessing.[2] When we meditate, we can arouse the kundalini to such an extent that it can activate the Leydig "control valve," allowing the energy to move throughout the other centers, stimulating their energies to manifest our conscious and subconscious images more rapidly and effectively. If the energy activates unbalanced centers and selfish or negative images, it can create great inner disharmony, mental problems, physical illness, or other difficulties. If our thoughts are loving, unselfish, and in harmony with God, the centers are balanced and the kundalini force flows smoothly to join the divine energy of the highest center, resulting in creativity, blessings, and healing to ourselves and to those for whom we pray.

Until we spiritualize and perfect our natures, eliminating our selfish thoughts and actions, we have two safeguards to help us balance the tremendous energy of the kundalini force: the Lord's

---

2. The Leydig "control valve" can be forcibly activated, allowing the misdirection of the kundalini force. This can occur through trauma, physical injury, or the abuse of alcohol or drugs (including LSD, peyote, marijuana, heroin, and, at times, certain prescription or over-the-counter drugs), resulting in hallucinations, mental confusion, sexual problems, nervousness, or physical deterioration.

Prayer and a spiritual Ideal.[3] (More information on these safeguards will be given throughout this chapter.) Then as we meditate, we gradually balance the energies of the endocrine system. This doesn't happen all at once. It is a step-by-step process that can take months, years, or lifetimes, depending on the application of divine love in the life of an individual.

Every seven years we regenerate new bodies through cell renewal. A person meditating on higher spiritual laws during this time can build a healthy body, find harmony within, and share God's light with the world. Someone meditating on worldly or selfish things for seven years could become like Frankenstein— one totally involved in creating through the mental and physical realms, without having spiritual awareness.

Understanding the Mind

The mind shares in both spiritual and physical activity, so it is important to understand how the mind works. Since it performs many important functions, we give it three labels to help us understand how it operates: the *conscious* mind, the *subconscious* mind, and the *superconscious* mind.

The conscious mind is involved in thinking and in understanding information presented to it through the physical senses. For example, we are using the sense of sight to perceive this printed information, so we use the conscious mind as we read.

The skills we gained in learning to read are stored in our subconscious, so they help us assimilate this written word, too. The subconscious is the storehouse of all that we have ever thought, felt, or done. Also, the subconscious mind controls the physical body's functions (heartbeat, digestion, etc.) so we won't have to think about our heartbeats or our breathing in order to continue functioning.

The superconscious is the God-mind within us, the spiritual part that is still at one with the wholeness that is God. This is the portion of the mind we seek to contact in meditation.

Understanding the Spirit and Soul

The spirit is the God-part of us and of everything else—the energy, the life. It is part of the trinity of the soul (spirit, mind, will). Each of us is a soul living in a physical body. The physical body is only the temporary home of the soul, for the body may

---

3. A spiritual Ideal is one based on a pattern of unselfishness and love in harmony with the teachings and life of the Christ. In the Cayce readings this image or pattern is called the "mark of the Lamb" (281-13). The "mark of the beast" is an image of selfishness. When raised within, it brings destructive influences into our lives. See Revelation 13-14.

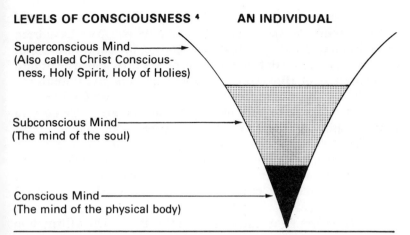

LEVELS OF CONSCIOUSNESS [4] **AN INDIVIDUAL**

Superconscious Mind————→
(Also called Christ Consciousness, Holy Spirit, Holy of Holies)

Subconscious Mind————————→
(The mind of the soul)

Conscious Mind————————————
(The mind of the physical body)

die, but the soul is eternal. At death, the soul is disconnected from
the body and freed from earthly limitations to experience other
states of consciousness. Meditation prepares the soul for its
continuing journey.

Preparation for Meditation

Physical Preparation

There are many ways to prepare for meditation. Some people
prefer to avoid certain activities (such as heavy exercise, eating,
sexual contact, etc.) before meditating. Others prepare by
bathing, chanting, inhaling incense, lighting candles, or listening
to music. Many do breathing exercises. Still others need little
physical preparation. They just become quiet and go within. All
of us prepare in our own ways, according to our own inner
concepts of "purification."

Mental Preparation

Our thoughts have the power to create. Our every thought is a
blessing or a curse to ourselves and others. Whatever we image or
concentrate on, good or bad, positive or negative, we will
eventually experience. We need to let go of negative or selfish
thoughts before we meditate, for they will keep us from reaching
the higher vibrations of true oneness with God.

Spiritual Preparation

The spirit is always seeking to express its real relationship with
God. However, some of us have so abused our bodies and minds

---

4. Drawing based on the educational aids originated by Herbert B. Puryear, Ph.D.,
President of Atlantic University; Association for Research and Enlightenment, Inc.

that our spirits are limited in their expressions. If we have the habit of thinking, speaking, and acting selfishly, we have been programming ourselves negatively, cutting off our awareness of God. Sweet incense or beautiful music can't lift a selfish heart into an awareness of Him. Only when we think and live unselfishly, lovingly, can we experience true at-one-ment with God.

To start us on the path of realizing at-one-ment, we need to have a spiritual Ideal. It should express the highest, most unselfish purpose we can imagine for our lives. It is the pattern we use to measure our thoughts and actions. As our minds, wills, purposes, and activities become more at one with the Ideal, we are guided to reach the consciousness of the Christ. (Lesson 3 explains the Ideal.)

At the beginning of each lesson in this book is an affirmation that will help us attune to a spiritual Ideal. When we meditate we can say the affirmation several times to focus our attention on it. Then, mentally, we repeat the affirmation until we feel the essence of its meaning.[5] Then we mentally release the affirmation to enjoy communion with God. (We can do this individually, or with a group.) If our minds wander, we gently return our focus to the affirmation until we once more feel the joy of communing with God.

The Lord's Prayer is recommended in the Cayce readings as an ideal prayer affirmation to use before meditation. It helps us raise an unselfish image, balancing our minds and bodies for meditation. When we pray "Our Father," we recognize the Fatherhood of God and the brotherhood of all mankind, the presence of God in everyone. "Hallowed be Thy name" affirms our reverence for God's power. "Thy kingdom come. Thy will be done in earth, as it is in heaven" reveals our desire to let God work through us and expresses our willingness to *live* according to His spiritual law, here and now. "Give us this day our daily bread" signifies our faith that God daily supplies our physical energy and material needs. "Forgive us. . . as we forgive our debtors" shows that we recognize the law of karma—that we are forgiven in the same way that we forgive others. (See Matthew 6:14-15.) "Lead us not into temptation" helps us recognize that we can live selfishly if we choose, or we can follow God's wise guidance. "But deliver us from evil" indicates that we want God's help to cleanse our minds, heal our bodies, and transform our lives. "For Thine is the

---

5. If an affirmation seems too long, we can capture its essence in a few words, or even one word in some cases. Our own shortened version may help us increase our concentration, thus leading to a higher awareness while shutting out mental distractions.

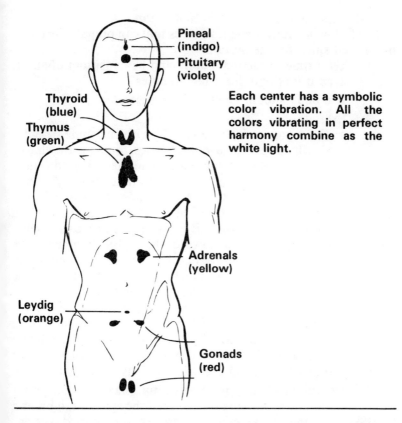

Pineal (indigo)

Pituitary (violet)

Thyroid (blue)

Thymus (green)

Adrenals (yellow)

Leydig (orange)

Gonads (red)

Each center has a symbolic color vibration. All the colors vibrating in perfect harmony combine as the white light.

kingdom, and the power, and the glory" reminds us that God is the spiritual essence within us, that we want His power to work through us, and that we want to share His blessings with others.

Each portion of the Lord's Prayer relates to one of our seven spiritual centers, as shown below.

> Our Father which art in *heaven* (Pituitary),
> Hallowed be thy *name* (Pineal).
> Thy kingdom come. Thy *will* (Thyroid) be done in earth, as it is in heaven.
> Give us this day our daily *bread* (Gonads).
> And forgive us our *debts* (Adrenals), as we forgive our debtors.
> And lead us not into *temptation* (Leydig), but deliver us from *evil* (Thymus):
> For Thine is the *kingdom* (Thyroid), and the *power* (Pineal), and the *glory* (Pituitary), for ever. Amen.

A Step-by-Step Guide for Meditation

The following outline suggests steps that can prepare the body, mind, and spirit for meditation:

1. Set a time to meditate daily and be consistent about it, even if it is only for a few minutes.

2. The body should be clean and relaxed.

3. Exercises:

    a. Head and neck exercise—Sit with the spine straight. Slowly lower the head three times, touching the chin to the chest. Return the head to an erect position, then lower it toward the back three times (slowly). Then return the head to the erect position and move it sideways toward the left shoulder three times, keeping the face to the front. Repeat these same movements, moving the head toward the right shoulder three times. Do these movements slowly and without lifting the shoulders. Now, slowly rotate the head clockwise three times; then counterclockwise three times.

    b. Breathing exercise—Inhale through the right nostril (holding left nostril with right index finger) and exhale through the mouth. Do this three times. Then inhale through the left nostril (holding right nostril with right thumb), exhaling each time through the right nostril.

4. Sit still with the spine straight but relaxed. Some prefer to lie down. In lying down, keep the spine straight, and cover the solar plexus (abdomen) with clasped hands.

5. Remove all negative thoughts or emotions through prayer, and center self in the spiritual Ideal and protective Light of the Christ.

6. Say the Lord's Prayer aloud or silently. (This can be done individually or with a group.)

7. Use an affirmation to focus the mind on God and prevent its wandering. If distracting thoughts occur, return the mental focus to the affirmation. Then let go of all thoughts to enjoy the Silence, the attunement with God.

Meditation Experiences

Each of us experiences the vibrations of meditation differently, depending on individual development. Some feel that they are swaying; others experience a pounding sensation in the lower spine or lower body. Some feel sensations of heat or cold. Others feel nothing at all, and that is normal, too. When we have a spiritual Ideal, truly seeking to be at one with God, we have no reason to be concerned about any sensations or lack of them. Instead of concentrating on distractions—visual, mental, or vibrational—we need to focus our minds on our spiritual Ideal or affirmation.

As we become one with the creative force of God's love, we enter the Holy of Holies, the place within where God communicates with us.[6] We experience peace, joy, new strength, a greater understanding of ourselves, and a more loving attitude toward others.

Conclusion

God always desires our companionship. We never need to feel afraid, unworthy, or unclean, for God is love; He always forgives our mistakes and seeks to help us. However, *He can help us only in proportion to our willingness to receive His help.*

If we want to improve our lives, we have to begin where we are. We have to face our current conditions and master them, or our next set of circumstances can be worse than our present one. Our problems are not outside us—they are within. Our solutions are also found within; for when we commune with God's inner presence, His wisdom guides us.

We can commune with God through meditation as we:
1. Desire to meet God within;
2. Believe and have faith that we can reach Him;
3. Make daily efforts to pray and meditate;
4. Live a spiritual Ideal the best we can, as we think, speak, and act.

Individual Growth Experiences

When we study and learn spiritual truths, we need to apply them in our lives or we can create problems for ourselves, for we are responsible for what we know. Below are listed suggested activities.
1. Keep a chart for the next four weeks, checking off the items as you apply them daily. Following is a sample chart for one week. Make four copies. Beneath the chart is an explanation of each activity.

---

6. I Corinthians 6:19 tells that the body is the temple of God. The Israelite temple was a symbol of the whole person: outer court (physical body); inner court, or Holy Place (mind); and Holy of Holies, or Most Holy Place (spirit). The ritual in the tabernacle or temple symbolized the way of attaining awareness of God. Exodus 26:30-35; Hebrews 9.

Day	Set/Review Ideal	Apply Ideal	Spiritual Reading	Spiritual Cleansing	Meditation Aids	Prayer	Same Time/Place	Pray for Others
Sun.								
Mon.								
Tues.								
Wed.								
Thurs.								
Fri.								
Sat.								

a. Set or Review Ideal—What has been your main goal in life? Do you have a spiritual Ideal? What is it? Be honest with yourself. (The Ideal may change as you grow spiritually.) What are your goals? Write a letter to yourself, expressing your goals. Change or rewrite them if you like. Are your goals in harmony with a spiritual Ideal?

b. Apply Ideal—At least once during the day, apply your Ideal to a situation. This could be as simple as smiling at others, being cheerful in a difficult situation, or praising others when you are tempted to criticize them.

c. Spiritual Reading—Before meditating, read uplifting or spiritual material. This could include poetry, the Bible, or other spiritually oriented books.

d. Spiritual Cleansing—Think of the people who have hurt you or made you angry. As you pray, forgive yourself, forgive the other people, and ask and know you have received God's forgiveness. God always forgives! Also, be willing to look at your faults through God's eye of mercy and love.

e. Meditation Aids—Some people need meditation aids; others do not. However, you may like to try some of these pre-meditation activities:
(1) Chant, using these syllables: "Ar-r-r—Ou-u-Ur-r," "Ar-r-r-r-r-AR," or "Aa-ree-ooh-mm."
(2) Listen to beautiful, soothing music.
(3) Burn incense or a scented candle.

f. Prayer—Use the Lord's Prayer and then pray in your own words if you like.

g. Same Time/Place—Choose the same time and, if possible, the same place to meditate daily.

h. Pray for Others—Pray for other people after you meditate. Do not describe what should be done in their lives; merely love them and ask God to help them at the level of their own needs. Be willing to do your part to help others.

It is a good idea to keep a journal of ideas, inspirations, and the results you obtain from following the above suggestions. It may help you find the preparation that works best for you.

2. Listed below are seven basic types of prayer. Each type may be used alone or in combination with one or more of the others as a helpful guide to prayer. Choose one or more of the types listed below and write a prayer-letter to God.

   a. Praise—a statement praising God. The Biblical Psalms have many beautiful examples.

   b. Thanksgiving—a way of realizing our many blessings as we give thanks for them often.

   c. Submission or Humility—giving our wills to God, focusing on our Ideal.

   d. Petition—an affirmation that God is our supply and is presently fulfilling all our needs.

   e. Guidance—an affirmation that we are being led throughout the day in each activity.

   f. Forgiveness or Confession—forgiving others of seeming slights or "wrongs" against us. It also includes self-forgiveness through accepting God's forgiveness for our shortcomings.

   g. Intercession—prayer for others. We pray and direct love and light to those we know need help. We do not specify details unless requested to do so by the person in need.

   An example using all seven steps:

Lord, how beautiful and wonderful is Your presence in everyone and everything. I thank you for strength, home, family, and friends. You are in charge of my life as I focus on the Christ. You fulfill my every need. Lead me every moment today so I may show others Your love. I forgive those who do not understand me, and I accept Your loving forgiveness for any part I played that may have contributed to their lack of understanding. I send Your loving light to my family, and especially to _____ , who has asked that I pray for him to be healed. Amen (which means so be it, or let it be).

Study Group Activities

1. Let the group discuss steps a-h of #1 above. Encourage the members to keep a journal for at least two weeks. At the next two meetings let them discuss insights they receive.

2. Let members write prayer-letters to God, individually or as a

group. (See #2 above.) Use their group effort or individual prayers before meditation at one of the meetings. Let each member pray a sentence or two.

3. *Bulletin Board Project.* Keep your handwork, poetry, prayers, etc., from this chapter and future chapters, on a bulletin board at home. You may purchase one, or if you prefer, you may make one instead.

Materials: 18″ x 24″ piece of heavy cardboard (corrugated). This is a good size for later framing.

Thumbtacks, scissors, and cord or twine. Cloth—preferably burlap or heavy cotton. Use a favorite solid color.

Cut the material to extend 2″ beyond the edge of the cardboard. Fold material over the edges, attaching it to the back of the cardboard with thumbtacks. If you prefer, put thumbtacks on the front edge and fringe the material edges instead of folding them over. Attach the cord to the back with thumbtacks.

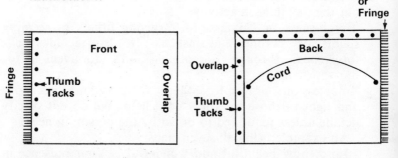

4. Go through magazines and cut out pictures that remind you of the beauty of meditation. Share your pictures with each other. Discuss what they mean to you. Put them on your bulletin boards to remind you to meditate.

Lesson 1
COOPERATION

Bible Verse: "...you should all be of one mind, living like brothers with true love and sympathy for one another..."(I Peter 3:8, PB)

Prayer Affirmation: Lord, I want to do Your will, not mine, and channel Your blessings to everyone. Let all I think and do be in such harmony with You that when You call on me, I can say, "Here I am, Lord. Send me; use me." (Based on Cayce reading 262-1; see also Isaiah 6:9.)

Introduction

Cooperation is God's basic law of harmony. We see it at work in the universe; the planets and stars move in harmony with divine plan. We see cooperation at work on earth with the orderly changing of the seasons. What chaos there would be without it! The planets would collide, the sun's light would fail, there could be no seasons, and soon no life could survive on earth.

Cooperation is important not only in the universe, but in every group effort. Without it plans fail, corporations fall, and schools become ineffective. It takes cooperation for nations, organizations, and families to live in peace.

Cooperation is important in our individual lives, too. On a physical level, even our good health depends on the many body parts working together harmoniously. On a spiritual level, cooperation is living in harmony with God's will. On an interpersonal level, cooperation is living in harmony with God's other children. When we truly cooperate we get our pride, our egos, out of the way so that God's love can flow through us to bless and uplift those we meet at home, school, work or play.

If we fail to cooperate, we create problems for ourselves because of the law of *karma*. Karma is the law of cause and effect, "sowing and reaping," or *receiving back what we think, say, or do* (Galatians 6:7). Jesus was referring to this law when He said, "For as you judge others, so you will yourselves be judged, and

15

whatever measure you deal out to others will be dealt back to you." (Matthew 7:2, NEB) We will be treated the same way we treat others, either in this life or in another lifetime. If we want to live, we must allow others to live. If we want to be forgiven, we have to forgive others (Matthew 6:14, 15). If we want cooperation, we must cooperate. When our thoughts and actions are loving and unselfish, we fulfill the law of karma through love (grace)—God's highest law (Romans 13:10).

If we don't cooperate with God's law of love, we eventually live in the inner and outer disharmony of mental confusion, physical disease, or problems in our relationships with others. We find the best in life when we cooperate with other people rather than trying to "get the best" of them—and others are helped, too.

How to Cooperate

God's creative force always expresses perfect harmony. To discover whether or not we are allowing His harmony to work in our lives, we can start by examining our thoughts and actions to see if they are cooperating with His law of love.

Our thoughts are especially important, for they affect the quality of our lives. They can become crimes or miracles as we put them into action. Let's be honest with ourselves as we look at our thought habits. What do we really think of ourselves? How do we view others? If we are resentful, critical, vengeful, hurt, or depressed, we aren't cooperating. If we can't follow the law of cooperation in our *thoughts,* we can't help other people and we keep others from helping us. Even Jesus couldn't help some people. Their negative thinking and lack of faith prevented His action in their lives (Matthew 13:58).

Next, we need to examine our actions. How do we treat others? Are our words critical? Do we argue with others often? Do we always want to have our way? Is our home life pleasant, or is it filled with bickering and suffering? When we are away from home, do we cause problems for teachers, sales clerks, waitresses, etc.? Let's bring our words and actions into harmony with God's law of love.

We start learning to cooperate when we truly begin to follow the pattern of Jesus Christ. His life was one of unity of purpose, thought and action within the will of God—perfect cooperation. He was unselfish and loving. When we make our minds one with His, we are truly cooperating. At first we may merely touch His creative force as we meditate. Later, as we begin to understand His law of love and try to apply it, we experience His force more fully. Finally, when we can totally *live* love, we, too, have the mind of Christ, complete oneness with His creative power (Philippians 2:5).

When we completely follow the Christ path, we think and act positively. The negative, selfish lower nature is healed, lifted up, and overcome. We are aware that all people are one in Him (I Corinthians 12:12-27). We love others, however we find them, just as they are. We treat others the way *we* wish to be treated (Luke 6:31). We think and speak kindly of everyone—even those who hurt us (Luke 23:34). We forget ourselves and do whatever is necessary to bring light, strength, health and understanding to others. We let God's love flow through us to others in even the small acts of kindness that may lift their burdens. As channels of His blessings, we bring hope, peace, and understanding to others in the hope not only that they will benefit, but that they will share these blessings with those around them in an unending chain reaction of love.

Few of us can live cooperation immediately. Most of us accomplish it a little at a time, step by step. Our first attempts at consciously applying cooperation may make us feel restless, confused, guilty, impatient, or overwhelmed by our failures. Dwelling on our problems only creates even more disharmony within. Instead, we need to change our attitudes to a positive focus, viewing ourselves through the loving and forgiving eye of God. He is always with us, guiding and helping us. We need only to commune with Him through prayer and meditation to be revitalized and rebalanced by His love. Also, the Christ is always ready to help us. He said that whatever we ask in His name (meaning within the harmony of His law of love) shall be done (John 14:14). He fully shares His power, strength, joy, abundance, light, and peace with us as we seek to apply cooperation in our lives.

Conclusion

As we learn to cooperate, we know we are one with God and we have a greater understanding of His universal creative force. We have more perfect minds and bodies. We are active channels of God's blessings to restore harmony to the earth and all its creatures. We are no longer interested only in ourselves; we find peace through becoming better friends and neighbors, serving other people. We discover the joyful purpose of helping Christ Jesus restore mankind to harmony with God.

1. Unscramble each set of letters to form a common word. Fill each blank with a letter.

W	E	P	O	R

(○)				(○)

M	S	O	N	O

	(○)	(○)	(○)	

T	O	B	N	E	N

	(○)			(○)	(○)

N	A	H	I	C

(○)		(○)	(○)	

Everything's in gear.

Next, print the circled letters here:

Now unscramble the circled letters to find the answer suggested by the drawing above. Place your completed word here:

2. Is there someone you dislike? A teacher? A classmate? A relative? A co-worker? If there is, find ten things you could like about him or her. Think of the good points (neat, pretty eyes, nice hair, etc.) List them below.

Do you see this person often? If you do, decide to smile at him

18

or her *every* time you meet. To help you do this, think about the good points you listed. After a few smiling encounters, ask yourself: "Do I feel different about this person now? Is the person friendlier?" If you are in a study group, share your experiences with the other members.

3. Do something nice for another person each day for a week without letting *anyone* know about it. This is really a challenge to your imagination. Hints: kind words, a loving prayer, an extra chore, a friendly visit with someone who needs a friend, etc.

Study Group Activities

1. Do #1 above.
2. Do #2 above. Let the group share insights.
3. Plan a group social, such as a picnic or a party, at which you will be eating a meal together. Have each person volunteer to bring a dish of food to share.
4. Using materials already at home, let each member make a small gift to take to the group. Plan this activity ahead of time, and have all bring their gifts at one time. Each person should put his gift in a brown paper bag, so no one can guess who brought it. Put the gifts on a tray and let each member choose one. Ideas: a rock painted with acrylic or poster paint; a plastic flower arrangement; macrame; drawing; candles; collage. (P.S. Don't let anyone know who made the gifts.)

Answers to Individual Growth Experiences #1:

COOPERATION
CHAIN
BONNET
MOONS
POWER

Lesson 2
KNOWING OURSELVES

Bible Verse: "Now you are the body of Christ and individually members of it." (I Corinthians 12:27, RSV)

Prayer Affirmation: Father, as we seek to know You, may we know ourselves as You know us, Your children of light. Then we can more fully share with others the light of Your Spirit. (Based on Cayce reading 262-5.)

Introduction

"Who am I?" is the question many of us keep asking. If we aren't aware of our complete history as children of God, co-creators with Him, and dwellers on this planet for many lifetimes, it's because we have lost conscious contact with the information stored in our souls (called *akasha* or the book of life—see Revelation 5:1-9; 20:12). The adventure of self-awakening, or discovering this information, is a step-by-step process achieved through prayer, meditation, and unselfish living. Until we can reach the enlightening moment of personal soul remembrance, the information from the Cayce readings can help us gain insights concerning the nature of our being.

Who Are We?

Each of us is a soul entity made up of spirit, mind, and will, housed in a physical body. The spirit is made in the image of the Creator and lives in constant companionship with Him. The mind has the ability to create through its thoughts. Each soul has free will and can choose to make its mind aware or unaware of the spirit. When it is involved in its own selfish thought creations, the mind closes off its awareness of the spirit. When the soul entity chooses to think and act in harmony with God's wholeness, it becomes completely aware of its oneness with the Creator. Until an entity realizes at-one-ment, it has the opportunity to

20

reincarnate in the earth lifetime after lifetime so that it may find perfect harmony with God.

The physical body is only the temporary home of the soul. At death, the soul leaves the body to experience other planes of existence and assimilate the lessons learned on earth. Although there are many mansions, or many dwelling places, beyond the earth plane, it is on earth that the soul finds the opportunity to fully perceive, apply, and understand the lessons that can restore it to perfect harmony with God.[1]

The physical body is the temple or residing place of the soul while on earth. Each body part has its own important job to help us function in the earth plane: the brain helps us channel and record our thoughts and actions; the nervous system distributes the electrical impulses to activate the body; the bones supply substance and rigidity; the joints and muscles allow mobility; the endocrine system channels and balances the God-Force of life and energy throughout the physical system. The senses make us aware of the needs and desires of the body, reacting according to the way we have programmed them. Impressions received and expressed by the senses are the results of more than one life experience.

All thoughts, experiences, and desires are recorded in the mind of the soul and reflected in the body's characteristics, activities, and facial features. Sometimes, for a while, people may be able to hide selfish attitudes and look beautiful on the outside, but eventually their real intentions will show. A person with spiritual perception can see people's real motives, no matter how hard they try to hide them. Jesus had this ability. (See Matthew 23:27-28.)

As we begin to know ourselves, the body, mind, and spirit will each experience an awakening. We have a physical awakening when we are fully aware of our physical desires and hungers. If we satisfy these selfishly, we sin, limiting or cutting off our awareness of God and communion with Him. This is symbolized in the Bible story of Adam and Eve: "When the woman saw that the fruit of the tree was good for eating. . .she took of its fruit and ate. . ." (Genesis 3:6, *Torah*) Then Adam also submitted to his desires,

---

1. See John 14:2 and II Corinthians 12:2. These Scriptures indicate different heavens or dwelling places in consciousness in the afterlife. The Cayce readings refer to many planes of awareness. These planes range from the highest level of perfect, blissful union with God, to lower ones described by various religions as "astral realm," "purgatory," or "hell." The word "hell" in the Bible is often a poor translation of the Hebrew and Greek words *(sheol, hades)*, meaning death or the realm of the dead. The Hebrew *geenna* (or *gehinnom*), meaning valley of sorrows, is also translated "hell" in the Bible. Whatever their labels, the lower levels are for meeting and cleansing any selfish attitudes or desires.

and both he and Eve were cast out of the Garden—the level in consciousness where they could freely commune with God.

A mental awakening takes place when we become aware that our minds can control our physical desires. An example of this is Daniel: "But Daniel resolved that he would not defile himself with the king's rich food, or with the wine which he drank. . ." (Daniel 1:8, NCE) Daniel controlled his physical desires, following his inner guidance concerning what he should eat and drink, even though his refusal of the king's rich food endangered his life.

We have a spiritual awakening when we are aware that the inner spirit of ourselves, others, and everything is really one. Jesus expressed this awareness when He said, "I and my Father are one," (John 10:30, RSV) and also when He said, " 'Inasmuch as ye have done it unto the least of these my little ones, ye have done it unto me.' " (Cayce reading 262-21; see also Matthew 25:35-40.) Jesus perfectly expressed His spiritual awakening in His daily life among men. We, too, will experience such an awakening when we daily live the Christ pattern; for through prayer, meditation, and the application of love in our activities, our communion with God grows and develops to perfect awareness of at-one-ment. Then we are freed from our entrapment in materiality and we overcome the earth, even as Jesus did.

Knowing Ourselves

We know ourselves and understand all three levels of our being as we give up our selfishness, our only block to complete self-understanding. As we inspect ourselves to relinquish all selfishness, we may discover that we are unaware of the areas of our self-centeredness. Our attitudes toward others can provide us with clues to help us see ourselves. If we see beauty in other people, we see a reflection of our own good qualities (Titus 1:15). If we are upset by others' negative words or actions, we may be reacting to traits that we ourselves possess. For example, if gossip is irritating us, we need to review our own words. If we have been guilty of gossiping, we can decide to stop. Then we can go within and forgive those involved, and accept God's forgiveness for our own shortcomings.

Daily, we should examine ourselves and mentally review the events of the past twenty-four hours. We should ask ourselves, "What did I say or do today? Why did I act the way I did? Would I have acted in front of God the way I acted before my brother?" Then we should resolve to make the Christ our standard for measuring what we think, say, and do. He taught us to follow only one law: "Love the Lord your God with all your heart, with all your soul, and all your strength, and with all your mind; and your neighbor as yourself." (Luke 10:27, NEB) When Christ's love is our standard for living, we can begin to channel God's blessings to others through our thoughts, words, and actions; for loving others is showing love for God.

As we turn to God through daily prayer and meditation, think and live His law of love, and serve others, we become God-centered instead of self-centered. God guides us to realize our true identities. We discover that we are His children and that His "I AM" is the center of our being (Exodus 3:13, 14; Psalms 82:6). We understand that God is in us and with us, wherever we are (Psalms 139:8).

Conclusion

Throughout the ages our thoughts, heredity, environment, karma, and activities in other planes of existence have been forming our individualities. What we are now is the result of what we have thought and done in every state of consciousness throughout the ages. Whatever we have concentrated on we have created, and we have to meet it here on earth or in other realms of existence. The direction we choose to go on earth we will continue to follow even after death. It is through earthly existence that we have the opportunity to redirect our lives through *applying* love. Therefore, each lifetime is a chance to change our existence for the better and to reawaken our awareness of oneness with God. Whatever we choose to think and do now is creating our futures. We can use our wills to separate ourselves from awareness of God or to realize our oneness with Him and work in divine harmony with His other children. We can cooperate with His unchangeable law of love, or we can struggle against it, meeting our own negativities and creating suffering for ourselves. Which will we choose?

We need to examine our goals in life. Do we live to satisfy our physical hungers? Do we want only to gain power, position, or wealth? Do we consider developing only the intellect as the highest attainment in life? Or do we wish to retreat from life, avoiding our responsibilities and opportunities? Have we avoided knowing God and finding our true selves so that we could continue to have our own ways, living in the physical consciousness, separated from the awareness of Him? We can shut God out, or we can attune to Him and realize our true heritage. Once we make the decision to seek Him, the Christ will help us and guide us along the way. He will lead us to know all about ourselves and who we really are—God's children, co-creators with His Spirit, and co-inheritors of His Kingdom (John 14:26; Romans 8:17).

Individual Growth Experiences

1. For two weeks keep a pad and pencil by your bed and record your dreams on awakening. Try to analyze them, for they can help you know yourself. Books that are helpful are *Dreams—Your Magic Mirror* and *Dreams, the Language of the Unconscious.* These may be ordered from the A.R.E. Press, P.O. Box 595, Virginia Beach, Virginia 23451.

2. Each evening for two weeks think back to a pleasant or unpleasant situation during the day. Pretend you are another person who was there at the time. See how you looked, spoke, and acted. Write about the situation.

   Answer these questions:

   (1) Why did I act the way I did?

   (2) How would Jesus have acted in this situation?

   (3) Did my words and actions show my love for God?

   This is a good exercise to repeat periodically. If you like what you see, you know you are living close to your spiritual Ideal. If you don't like the way you are acting, decide to replace the negatives with positives by praying for God's help; re-enacting the scene in your mind and acting the way God would want you to; and forgiving everyone involved, including yourself. If the problem recurs, you will be prepared to react in a loving way.

3. Pretend that you are Jesus. Remember His love for you and for everyone. Write a letter to yourself from Jesus. Through His eyes tell of your good qualities. What words of comfort would He say to you? What would He want you to do with your life? How would He want you to act? Then reread your letter. Does it really sound like Jesus? Meditate. Feel Christ's love flow through you.

Study Group Activities

1. Have the group members do #1 above and discuss their dreams. Encourage them to analyze these, emphasizing the positive aspects. Remember to keep the comments gentle.

2. Have each member tell the group his or her astrological sun sign. Ask each to share the good qualities found in the sign. What are the negative traits? Does each person follow the

description of the sign? Encourage members to be independent of the influences of the sign by following the Christ's pattern of love. You may need an astrology book to look up the different sun signs. Some members might like to draw and color a symbol of the sign that pertains to them, or to cut one out of a magazine. These may be placed on bulletin boards.

3. Members can do Individual Growth Experiences #2 at home.

Lesson 3
WHAT IS MY IDEAL?

Bible Verse: "Let this mind be in you, which was also in Christ Jesus." (Philippians 2:5, KJV)

Prayer Affirmation: Merciful God, help me view others as You see them. Let me see You in everyone. (Based on Edgar Cayce reading 262-11.)

Introduction

In the previous lessons we have emphasized the importance of the ideal we have in life. Exactly what is an ideal? An ideal is the motive behind what we think and do—the pattern that we are using to measure and shape our lives. A spiritual Ideal is the highest pattern of perfection that we can imagine. It is an unselfish image of what we want to be like, something beyond us that we want to reach. A materialistic ideal is a life pattern based on the desires of the selfish, lower nature. *Consciously or unconsciously, we always have an ideal, whether it is spiritual or materialistic, and it is the force that directs our lives.*[1] Whatever the ideal, whatever the mind dwells on, we create, for mind is the builder. (Cayce readings 23-1, 197-1, 202-4, and many more)

Let's not confuse an idea or a goal with an ideal. An idea is a fleeting mental image, a thought. When we decide to pursue an idea, it can become a goal. A goal is something we want to accomplish, something we are working toward, but it isn't the pattern we use to measure the activities of our lives. Ideas and goals may lead us toward or away from the ideal. For example, we could imagine that Noah's ideal was communion with God and following His guidance. When God told Noah to build an ark, making a boat became Noah's goal. As he began to work toward his goal, he had ideas about how to follow God's instructions to construct the ark. His ideas and goal were in line with his ideal.

---

1. "...what we are—in any given experience, or time—is the combined results of what we have done about the ideals that we have set!" (Cayce reading 1549-1)

Therefore, Noah's ideal was spiritual, because it was an unselfish pattern for his life, centered in God. His goal and ideas worked in harmony with his Ideal, leading him toward even closer communion with God. (See Genesis 6-7.) We need to be sure that our ideal is a spiritual one and that our ideas and goals are in harmony with it.

Ideals Change as We Grow

As children we have simple ideas, goals, and ideals. Just as we grow physically and our thoughts and ideals change, our concepts of God change, too. (See I Corinthians 13:11-13.) As we mature spiritually, eventually we realize that God's Spirit is our Parent, that we are expressions of Him, and that we need His guidance. We seek an even closer communion with Him. As we do, the ideal changes from an immature, materialistic, intellectual, or selfish one to a loving, spiritual Ideal. If we refuse to grow spiritually, we allow our lives to be directed by a selfish ideal, creating problems for ourselves and those around us.[2]

The Perfect Spiritual Pattern

We find the perfect pattern for our life in the Christ, who is the Way. His life perfectly expresses the highest Ideal—the ultimate spiritual attainment that can be reached on earth. His teachings tell us the way to pattern our lives; His life of service to others shows us the way to apply the pattern to everyday situations. If He is our pattern and we follow His example of love and service, we will reach the Christ Consciousness. We will understand that all of God's children are one. Our physical and mental goals will so harmonize with the spiritual Ideal that our thoughts, words, and actions will bless all we meet. If we choose any other pattern than that lived and taught by the Christ, we cheat ourselves of the joy of the ultimate spiritual experience (John 10:1).

Formulating the Ideal

As we each choose the words which express the ideal we want to follow, we need to realize that:

". . .the gift of God to man is an *individual* soul that may be one *with* Him, and that may know itself to be one with Him and yet individual in itself, with the attributes *of* the whole, yet *not* the whole." (Cayce reading 262-11)

---

2. The Bible describes the results of selfishness: ". . .if you are guided by the Spirit you will be in no danger of yielding to self-indulgence. . .when self-indulgence is at work the results are obvious: fornication, gross indecency and sexual irresponsibility; idolatry and sorcery; feuds and wrangling, jealousy, bad temper and quarrels; disagreements, factions, envy; drunkenness, orgies and similar things." (Galatians 5:16, 19-21, JB)

Although each of us is an individual expression of the wholeness of God, one part is not the whole, for the rest of God's children make up the complete body of Christ (I Corinthians 12:12-27). Therefore, the ideal we choose should turn us *toward* others, not away from them. It should cause us to show mercy to other people, which in turn will allow us to accept God's mercy in our own lives (Matthew 5:7). Such an ideal leads us to a productive life filled with the "peace that passes understanding." (Philippians 4:7).

Now we should prayerfully choose a spiritual ideal, symbolize its meaning in three words or less, and write it down. Then we should choose the mental attitudes and physical activities that will harmonize with it. The chart on page 30 of this book will help us in this activity. It provides us with an opportunity to examine ourselves sincerely.

Attaining the Ideal

The more we commune with God and seek to live in harmony with others, the more our thoughts, words, and actions will conform to the spiritual Ideal in Him. Eventually, as we continue to follow the Ideal mentally and physically, we become one with it, living it constantly. When we do, we have the mind of Christ— total awareness of at-one-ment with God (Philippians 2:5).

If we falter, stumble, or make mistakes along the way, we need to realize that our errors serve to point out the important lessons we need to learn in this life. Instead of indulging in self-condemnation or blaming others, we should resolve even more firmly to do the best we can to express loving thoughts and actions. Then we should leave the results of our efforts with God. He always helps us along the way and rewards our every effort. Step by step He leads us to see the spirit in ourselves and in everyone. This frees us from being influenced by the criticism, opinion, or praise of ourselves or others that might divert us from being true to the Ideal.

The Christ, too, is always ready to aid us. He can calm our troubled minds, even as He quieted the stormy sea (Mark 4:39). His voice of love comforts us with His promise:

"Come to me, all of you who are weary and overburdened, and I will give you rest!" (Matthew 11:28, PB)

"Look, I am standing at the door, knocking. If one of you hears me calling and opens the door, I will come in and share his meal (portion), side by side with him." (Revelation 3:20, JB; authors' note in parentheses)

Individual Growth Experiences

The chart below is shaped like a target, signifying the Ideal toward which we are aiming. The center is the mark, the bull's eye we want to reach, our spiritual Ideal. The next level is the mental target, the highest mental attitudes we want to have toward four areas of our lives—home, school or work, ourselves, and others. The outer level is our physical target—the spiritual Ideal and positive attitudes put into action in the same four areas of our lives.

Instructions:

1. Pray to God asking for guidance to choose the three words or less that best describe the meaning of your personal spiritual Ideal. Meditate. Place the word or words in the center of the target, using a pencil.

2. List positive mental attitudes which can express your spiritual Ideal on the mental level. Be sure to take into special consideration any problems you may have in thinking positively about others. A helpful clue to self-inspection: The traits in others that cause you to have an emotional reaction may be mirrors of your own characteristics.

3. List physical applications in words or actions that can express the mental attitudes you listed.

4. Be sure to use a pencil. Your ideal may change as you mature spiritually, and you may want to make changes in your chart. Review your chart often to see how you are progressing and where you need to make changes.

Below is an example:

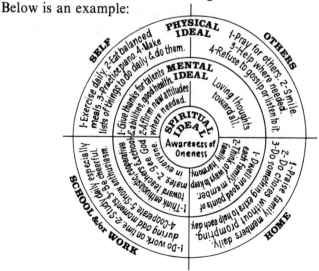

Now fill in your own chart:[3]

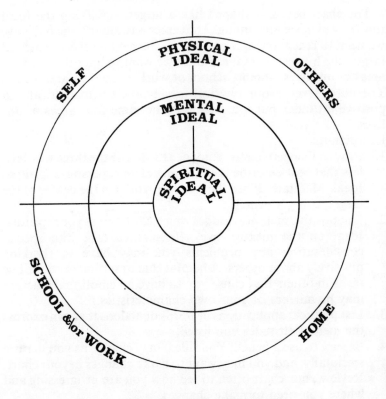

Study Group Activities

1. Filling in the above chart should be the main study group activity for this chapter. Before working on the chart, the group should discuss their childhood ideals and how they have changed. Then each person should be given the time to fill in his or her chart *privately*. Insights may be shared if members desire to do so. Encourage members to put charts in a convenient place for frequent review.

2. As an assignment, let each person choose a Bible verse, song, poem, symbol, or picture that best describes his or her Ideal. Bring chosen material to the next meeting to share with the group. These may be placed on bulletin boards as a reminder of the Ideal.

---

3. "Target" charts based on design originally used in *Meditation and the Mind of Man*, A.R.E. Press, 1975.

Lesson 4
FAITH

Bible Verse: "According to your faith be it done to you."
(Matthew 9:29, RSV)

Prayer Affirmation: O Lord, as I seek You, may my heart be pure,
so that I may be aware of the faith that lives within. Help me
express faith in You, in my neighbor, and in myself. (Based on
Cayce reading 262-13.)

What Is Faith?

Faith is a quality of the soul—the inner spiritual awareness that
God is always with us. Faith is knowing that we can contact His
inner creative force to make things happen in our lives. We create
through faith, for "Faith gives substance to our hopes. . ."
(Hebrews 11:1, NEB) Everything that has been created was
brought into being through faith.

Faith ". . .makes us certain of realities we do not see." (Hebrews
11:1, NEB) When we have faith, we are centered in the reality of
God's truths, making us sure and unafraid. We don't rely on
information from the senses, including knowledge and logic, for
these are tuned to the three-dimensional world, rather than to
higher spiritual laws. If we depend on sense data we have
confidence, not faith. When we have confidence alone, our senses
can confuse us, causing doubt, fear, and failure. Peter is an
example of a person who became deceived by his senses. In faith,
he began walking on the water to reach Jesus. But when he felt the
strength of the wind, he relied on the information of his senses
rather than on faith in the Christ. Doubt and fear crept in and he
began to sink (Matthew 14:28-31).

Making Faith Grow

Although faith is part of our divine heritage and is inherently
within us, few of us have learned to express it fully. It lies within,
seeking to be revealed, just as life's essence lies within a seed,

31

waiting to sprout and grow. We can stifle faith's activity in our lives and lose awareness of it, or we can encourage its expression. If we deny faith's existence, our doubts grow, and we can't receive the rewards of faith.

We release faith's creativity in our lives by acknowledging it and using it—by acting as though we have already received. For example, perhaps we have need of extra finances for a special project.[1] To have the faith to fulfill this need, first we should realize that God is with us, helping us. Then we pray and meditate, knowing that our request will be answered. Finally, we live and act as though the need has already been fulfilled. When the financial help comes, we should remember to express gratitude to God, and give His Spirit the credit. Jesus said, ". . .the Father that dwelleth in me, he doeth the works." (John 14:10, KJV)

Suppose our faith appears unfruitful and we do not receive the financial aid we sought? Then we need to examine carefully our motives, thoughts, and actions. Were our motives in harmony with a spiritual Ideal, or were they selfish? Selfishness confines us to the conscious mind and the confusion of the senses, limiting the expression of faith. Did we have faith-filled thoughts, or did we doubt or worry? Uncertain, wavering thoughts can cancel faith's activity. Were we as willing to give as to receive? If we don't give to others, we limit our own supply. Were our thoughts, words, and actions loving? If not, we prevented the full expression of God's power to make our faith active.

To activate the faith we need to meet life's conditions, we need to apply the lessons we have already learned. We should pray and meditate, cooperate, live in harmony with a spiritual Ideal, and reflect the truth of our divine nature in our lives. Living these lessons may seem to be only small expressions of faith, but every time we apply faith it becomes more active. As our faith grows and matures it becomes strong enough to meet life's greatest challenges. Our faith reaches its ultimate strength when we bring our thoughts and actions into perfect harmony with the Christ. When we do, we have the mind of Christ, and the faith to heal, change the future of nations, and even create new worlds.

The Importance of Faith

It takes faith to commune with God, conquer our inner fears

---

1. A good guide for increasing faith concerning finances is *Economic Healing*, by Economic Healing Group 1, available through A.R.E. Press, P.O. Box 595, Virginia Beach, VA 23451.

and confusions, and have good will toward others. It requires faith to turn within through prayer and meditation and listen for God's promptings of guidance. It takes even greater faith to follow what He tells us to do. It requires consistent faith to stay true to the Ideal, sacrificing all selfishness, so that we can experience complete at-one-ment with God.

Most of us concentrate on our physical or material problems when we should be more concerned with our mental attitudes, for thoughts have creative power. We can use the mind to alleviate physical pain or problems, but what can relieve our mental anguish? Only through faith in the truth of our spiritual natures can we have the self-understanding that makes us able to overcome our fears and confusions. As we turn to our Source within, we discover that we are not just "animal" or physical beings, but expressions of God and co-workers with Him. When we realize that God is the central core within us, we can't doubt ourselves; for if we do, we lack faith in God. He has promised that He will never leave us or desert us. (See Hebrews 13:5.) Through faith in Him we can affirm:

"I am not alone, because the Father is with me." (John 16:32, NEB)

"With the Lord to help me, I fear nothing . . ." (Hebrews 13:6, JB)

"There is nothing I cannot master with the help of the One who gives me strength." (Philippians 4:13, JB)

Through faith we can see God in our fellow men and have good will toward them. Although we may not always agree with others, we can realize that God is working through their lives, just as He is working through ours. Trusting people, even when outer appearances are against our doing so, is a measure of our faith in God. When we trust others, our thoughts and actions are more loving, and people tend to respond to us in the same way.

Where Are We Placing Our Faith?

Since all of us are God's offspring, we are His co-creators and have the power and free will to direct our lives. Whatever we have faith in, we create. Jesus expressed this when He said, "According to your faith be it done to you." (Matthew 9:29, RSV)

Whatever ideal we have will be expressed in our lives. Are we like primitive man, whose ideal is survival, seeking only the physical comforts of food, warmth, and shelter? Are we like philosophical man, seeking inner peace through the efforts of the intellect? Or is our ideal to live as spiritual man, looking beyond our selfish physical and mental drives to seek harmony with God and to express His love to our fellow men through service? Only faith in a spiritual Ideal can lead us into union with our Source and enable us to channel His help and inspiration to others.

Faith's Reward

Faith centered in God is limitless, and so are its rewards. However, our rewards depend on our use of faith. God has unlimited blessings and treasures for each of us who is willing to receive them. If we do not express faith, we prevent God's blessings from flowing through our lives. Even Jesus could not help some people in His own home town because of their lack of faith (Matthew 13:54-58). When we truly have faith in God, we can receive His blessings. He said, "Prove me. . .I will open up the windows of heaven for you and pour out a blessing so great you won't have room enough to take it in! Try it! Let me prove it to you!" (Malachi 3:10, LB)

Jesus' faith was so strong that He could still a storm, walk on water, heal and bless multitudes. When we express faith, we too can accomplish anything. Jesus told us that our faith can restore our sight, heal us, and make us whole—in other words, it can save.[2] (See Mark 5:34 and 10:52; Luke 7:44-50; and Ephesians 2:8.) He said, ". . .whatever you pray for in faith you will receive." (Matthew 21:22, NEB) Even a small amount of faith is powerful! The Christ said, ". . .if you have faith no bigger even than a mustard-seed, you will say to this mountain, 'Move from here to there!' and it will move; nothing will prove impossible for you." (Matthew 17:20, NEB)

When we have faith in the Christ, we have the peace and freedom we can find nowhere else. He has promised to be with us always (Matthew 28:20). United with Him through love, we can say with Paul:

". . .overwhelming victory is ours through him who loved us. For I am convinced that there is nothing. . .nothing in all creation that can separate us from the love of God in Christ Jesus our Lord." (Romans 8:38-39, NEB)

"I can do all things through Christ which strengtheneth me." (Philippians 4:13, KJV)

When we open ourselves to be God's channels of blessings, having faith in Him, He will work through us to overcome all our inner and outer struggles. His Holy Spirit will guide us to even

---

2. The word "save," *sozo*, means to save, deliver, protect, heal, preserve, do well, save (self), be whole.

deeper faith and the revelations of His Spirit of truth.[3]

"And what more shall I say? For time would fail me to tell of Gideon, Barak, Samson, Jephthah, of David and Samuel and the prophets—who through faith conquered kingdoms, enforced justice, received promises, stopped the mouths of lions, quenched raging fire, escaped the edge of the sword...And all these, though well attested by their faith, did not receive what was promised, since God had foreseen something better for us, that apart from us they should not be made perfect. Therefore, since we are surrounded by so great a cloud of witnesses, let us also lay aside every weight, and sin which clings so closely, and let us run with perseverance the race that is set before us, looking to Jesus the pioneer and perfector of our faith..." (Hebrews 11:32-34, 39-40; 12:1, 2, RSV)

Individual Growth Experiences

1. Open your Bible to the following verses and list some of the things that faith can do:

Mark 5:34	Acts 15:9
Mark 11:22-25	Romans 1:17
Luke 7:50	Galatians 3:9
Luke 8:24-25	Hebrews 11:3
Luke 12:28-31	Hebrews 11:5
Luke 18:42	James 1:3

   (See also the complete chapter of Hebrews 11.)
   A list is supplied at the end of this chapter, printed upside down.

2. Take two pots and fill them with potting soil. Plant a seed in each. Use marigolds, sunflowers, pinto beans, or any other fast-sprouting seed. Give both pots the same care, water, and light. Choose one plant to pray for to test your faith in prayer. Pray for the seed as you plant it. Pray for it daily. Tend to the other plant, too, but don't pray for it.
   At the end of a week, compare growth between the two plants. Make a simple chart showing height, number and size of leaves, and color. Check each week for a month. Did your faith and prayer have any effect on the plant? Was there any difference in the growth patterns of the two plants? If you are uncertain about the results, plant two other seeds and repeat the experiment.

---

3. See John 14:16, 26; 16:13.

Study Group Activities

1. Have the group members do #1 above. Form members into two or three groups; divide the Bible verses equally among the groups. Let them decide what faith does, according to the Biblical accounts. Encourage them to discuss insights.
2. Let the members do #2 above, individually or as groups. Let them compare experiences.
3. To demonstrate their faith in prayer, let the group members choose a time when they can pray and meditate each day, wherever they may be. Have everyone pray for one another each day at the same time. (Choose a time convenient for everyone.) Continue this for one month. At each meeting, have the members compare experiences of faith and prayer improving their lives. Did things go better when they prayed for others and received prayers? Could they feel each other's prayers? Encourage the members to continue their group prayer time on a regular basis.

Faith can: heal or make whole, move mountains, answer prayer, save (bring peace, wholeness, prosperity, healing), control the elements, supply our needs, restore sight, purify the heart or make it holy, reveal God, bring blessings, bring understanding, and help us to be patient.

Lesson 5

VIRTUE AND UNDERSTANDING

Bible Verse: "Finally, brothers, fill your minds with everything that is true, everything that is noble, everything that is good and pure, everything that we love and honor, and everything that can be thought virtuous or worthy of praise." (Philippians 4:8, JB)

Prayer Affirmation: O Lord, my Liberator and Defender, may I express virtue and understanding, that my heart may be pure and my prayers rise to You. (Based on Cayce reading 262-17.)

Introduction

Just as faith is a soul quality, so are virtue and understanding. Virtue is letting the Spirit of God work through us, making our motives, thoughts, and actions pure. When we lead lives of prayer, meditation, cooperation, knowing ourselves, having faith, and staying true to the Ideal, we are expressing virtue. In other words, virtue is living the fruits of the spirit: "love, joy, peace, patience, kindness, goodness, faithfulness, gentleness, self-control." (Galatians 5:22-23, RSV)

When we so live in virtue that it is built into our minds, we have understanding; for understanding is the reward of virtue. Understanding is experiencing the Creative Force and determining how Its laws work through the souls, minds, and bodies of men. It is realizing that we are part of God's laws and not just observers of them.

There is a difference between understanding and earthly knowledge.[1] Knowledge can be defined as the learning process that programs the conscious mind through the senses. Knowledge may reveal information about mathematics, astronomy, science, and other physical data. But understanding goes beyond the limitations of the senses to reveal God's spiritual laws.

1. The definition of earthly knowledge in this chapter should not be confused with the spiritual definition given in *A Search for God*, Book 2, in the chapter "Knowledge."

Understanding is eternal, but earthly knowledge changes with time and some day it will even pass away (I Corinthians 13:89). Knowledge can be helpful when it is in harmony with the Ideal. If it isn't, it can become a barrier that prevents spiritual growth.

Few who have earthly knowledge have understanding also. This explains why many experience miracles, but few understand them. Actually, miracles are not the breaking of known scientific laws; they are the fulfillment of spiritual laws. Jesus, who understood spiritual laws, did not consider His mighty works miraculous.

The Importance of Virtue and Understanding

It takes understanding to set goals in harmony with a spiritual Ideal, and it requires the purity and power of virtue to accomplish these lovingly. Although the goals arising from our Ideal may not be realized immediately, they may be reached a little at a time through daily applying the best we know. In this way, step by step, we improve the quality and productivity of our lives; for our loving intentions and activities are never lost, but are built into our souls and continue to be fruitful.

If we wish to live in harmony with other people, we need the understanding to choose the right course of action toward them. In some situations we may have empathy or insights in our dealings with others because we, too, have lived through similar situations. But if we have no common ground of experience, people's mistakes or actions may mystify us, tempting us to criticize or condemn them. Only through the guidance of God's Holy Spirit can we find the depth of understanding we need to react lovingly to all people. As we seek His help, He leads us to realize that He lives not only in us but within our burdened brothers. When we let God's Spirit of love and virtue flow through us to them in kind thoughts, words, and actions, we can bring harmony to our relationships with them. Our kind actions lift not only them, but ourselves, for ". . .he that approaches [heaven] must lean upon one [he has] helped." (Cayce reading 281-4)

We must express virtue and understanding to be effective in spiritual work, for we can only share with others what we ourselves are willing to live. Can we expect others to be virtuous if we are not? Can we look for others to seek understanding if we show no understanding ourselves? People judge us by what we say and do, so we must "practice what we preach," in order to lead others to truth.

Realizing Virtue and Understanding

Within all of us our souls have a deep desire to realize virtue and understanding. No matter how "out of tune" we get, eventually something—a song, a poem, a scripture, a kind word, a friendly act—inspires us to seek beyond our own selfish desires. Then we each cry, "Lord, help me to reshape and cleanse my life. Show me the way to find You, for my soul longs for You." (See Psalms 42:1.) When we really seek virtue and understanding, we know we will find them, for Jesus promised: ". . .seek, and you shall find; knock, and it shall be opened to you." (Luke 11:9, NCE)

We find virtue and understanding through faith—faith in God, faith in ourselves, and faith in others. It takes complete faith in God to enter the Holy of Holies through prayer and meditation and receive the deepest understanding of His Spirit. We also need to have faith in ourselves, faith in our inner purity, to let His Spirit express through us to purify our lives, reshaping them to the image of the Christ. We must also have faith in others—the faith that overlooks their faults and sees their inner purity. The Bible says, "To the pure all things are pure. . ." (Titus 1:15, RSV) As we have faith in the inner purity of others, *we* are freed to express the virtue we once demanded of *them*.

Jesus perfectly expressed virtue and understanding in His life among men, and we express these too when we follow His path. When we walk in the steps of the Christ we do God's will, not ours; we stay in tune with Him through prayer and meditation; we have an unselfish concept of our physical, mental, and spiritual needs. Our only purpose in reaching the Christ Consciousness is to do God's work and bring blessings to others. We will not allow ourselves to have unkind thoughts toward anyone, for we will view all people through God's eyes.

The Effects of Virtue and Understanding

When we have virtue we release a power greater than dynamite—the power of the Holy Spirit![2] It lends strength to our spiritual qualities, heightens our awareness of God, and increases the expression of our faith. The more we channel this power to bless others, the more it can work through us, becoming so strong that it makes seemingly impossible things happen. Also, the pure

---

2. See Mark 5:30 and Luke 6:19. These Scriptures in the *King James Version* of the Bible tell about "virtue" going out of Jesus to help and heal others. This word in Greek is *dunamis,* meaning force or power. Our English words dynamic, dynamo, and dynamite come from this same Greek word.

power of virtue defends and protects so that no harmful plan directed against us can survive.

Just as virtue is our defense, understanding is our weapon. When we direct understanding toward one who seeks to be our enemy, we see his real intention and purpose and we are able to conquer his harmful activities. But what is even more important, we have the understanding that makes us able to turn him into a friend. Understanding gives us the insight to solve our problems. Only when we have virtue and understanding are we able to rise above the struggles of life.

Conclusion

Every day we are building what we really are. We can compare our self-building to constructing a house. Are we choosing good building materials (qualities that help our growth)? Are we getting rid of imperfect materials (anything that hinders us from realizing at-one-ment with God)? Is the foundation sound (our Ideal centered in Christ)? Is the building straight (our life balanced and in line with the Christ Ideal)? Are we willing to be examined by the building inspector (God)? What we build depends on ourselves, not on anyone else. Are we building a shack, or a temple for the living God? (See I Corinthians 6:19-20; Ephesians 2:19-22.)

Whatever we build affects not only ourselves, but others, too. Our thoughts and actions affect those around us. Love, mercy, justice, patience and forgiveness *lived* are catching! Others will want to live them, too. When we really love others, we will experience the peace that comes from being in harmony with God's will. The materialistic values we once had won't interest us any more. The spiritual things we once tried to avoid will become what we cherish most. We will seek to live virtuously so that we can understand and work in harmony with God's laws. We will give thanks to God for the soul qualities we express as we are cleansed and purified by His Holy Spirit.

The Bible says:

". . .you will be able to share the divine nature and to escape corruption in a world that is sunk in vice. But to attain this, you will have to do your utmost yourselves, adding goodness to the faith that you have, understanding to your goodness, self-control to your understanding, patience to your self-control, true devotion to your patience, kindness to your fellow men to your devotion, and, to this kindness, love. If you have a generous supply of these, they will not leave you ineffectual or

40

unproductive; they will bring you to a real knowledge of our Lord Jesus Christ." (II Peter 1:4-8, JB)

Individual Growth Experiences

1. Choose one fruit of the spirit to live for one week: love, joy, peace, patience, kindness, goodness, faithfulness, gentleness, or self-control. (See Galatians 5:22, RSV.) Look for Bible verses or other inspirational materials that describe the quality you choose. Then write a positive prayer affirmation about this quality. Use your affirmation daily for one week. Were you able to express this quality? Was it easy? Was it hard? Where was it the easiest to live it? Where was it the hardest? Why?

2. *Haiku* is a simple Japanese poetic form. (It is pronounced high-coo.) It consists of three lines. The first line has five syllables, the second line has seven syllables, and the third line has five syllables. Write a *haiku* about the fruit of the spirit you choose to live for one week.
   Example:

Radiant flower	(5 syllables)
Lifts its lovely face to God,	(7 syllables)
Expressing His joy.	(5 syllables)
OR	
In faith I reach God.	(5 syllables)
He guides me with His Spirit	(7 syllables)
And brings me new peace.	(5 syllables)

Study Group Activities

1. Have the group do #1 above together. Let them share their Bible verses or other inspirational materials with the group. Have them share their experiences.

2. Have the group write the *haiku* poetry suggested in #2 above. If some of the members are musical, let them write music to fit the poetry. If some of them are particularly inventive, let them put the verses together to form stanzas of a song. Their efforts may be put on their bulletin boards.

Lesson 6
FELLOWSHIP

Bible Verse: "...if we walk in the light, as he is in the light, we have fellowship one with another..." (I John 1:7, KJV)

Prayer Affirmation: O Lord, how excellent is Your name, Your presence in everything and in everyone! Since You live in every person, I cannot hold negative feelings toward anyone without cutting off my communion with You. May I show love to everyone; for only then can my prayers and meditations reach You and I experience Your divine fellowship. (Based on Edgar Cayce reading 262-21; also see Psalms 8:1, 9.)

Introduction

Deep within, each of us has a yearning for the companionship we had with God at creation's beginning, when we all walked and talked with Him. We knew that we were one with God, with each other, and with all creation. Through selfishness we fell in consciousness and lost awareness of our fellowship with God and our brotherhood with each other. (See Genesis 3.)

Jesus Christ came to show us how to reawaken our companionship with God. He taught us that the way to fellowship with the Father is through the expression of loving brotherhood with one another. He viewed the relationship of God and man as interwoven and inseparable—like one piece of cloth. He described this close relationship when He said, "...I am in my Father, and you in me and I in you." (John 14:20, NEB) Therefore, showing love to others *is* expressing our love for God, which in turn allows us to draw closer to Him in companionship.

The brotherhood of man, then, is the reflection of man's inner fellowship with God. Brotherhood is the outer physical expression of our inner spiritual oneness with God, just as a wedding ring is an outer expression of the inner love and union of marriage. The more we live in brotherhood with man, the more complete is our fellowship with God.

Brotherhood with Others

Shortly after man's consciousness fell, he began to view others as separate from himself. He forgot that God lives in everyone. When this happened, his feeling of separation enabled him even to commit murder. The first person murdered, according to the Bible, was Abel, who was slain by his brother Cain. After Cain killed Abel and had to face God with his crime he asked, "Am I my brother's keeper?" (Genesis 4:9, *Torah;* see also I John 3:15-17.)

Today, many are still asking this same question, because "fallen" man doesn't want to accept his responsibility toward others. If we have so separated our awareness from God (sinned) that we, too, take no responsibility toward others, we will suffer. We will feel upset, depressed, and fearful—perhaps without even realizing why. Only when we love and serve others can we re-establish fellowship with them and with God, and experience peace.

"See what love the Father has given us. . ." (I John 3:1, RSV) God has only love for *all* of us and He never turns it off; He is always merciful (Psalms 106:1; Luke 6:36). Since God forgives us, can we fail to show the same mercy to others? If others have hurt us or caused us problems, we can patiently refuse to condemn or hold grudges, and continue to show love. If we truly love them, however, we do more than just ignore their faults—we see God within them. Then we can follow the Christ's teachings to ". . .do good to those who hate you; bless those who curse you; pray for those who treat you spitefully." (Luke 6:28, NEB; see also verses 29-31.)

When we live in fellowship we extend our friendship to others, too, offering them our help when they are tempted and our aid when they need it. We comfort them if they are sad and seek to calm them if they are angry. Our words are kind and sincere; yet we avoid flattery. We know that when we treat others as we would like them to treat us, we are not only helping them and, in turn, bringing blessings to ourselves; we are serving Our Lord, who said, ". . .as you did it to one of the least of these my brethren, you did it to me." (See Luke 6:31, NEB; Mark 4:24; Matthew 25:40, RSV; and Matthew 25:31-46.)

Expressing our brotherhood with other people includes respecting the law and keeping our commitments, for others are affected by our actions. Also, they evaluate our beliefs by the way we live them. We must not only live our beliefs, but have the courage to be willing to explain them in the face of criticism. Pure motives and actions in our relationships with others are essential for living in at-one-ment with them and with God.

Our Fellowship with God

If we want to know the depth of our relationaship with God, we need to examine our thought habits concerning ourselves and others. First, we should examine our attitudes about ourselves. If we are experiencing disharmony within or without, we are out of harmony with God. Inner confusion comes from a lack of faith in ourselves, and thus, in God, for His unlimited power lives within us. If we are experiencing guilt, worry, or anguish, we need only to turn within to our Source, relieving our anxiety through prayer and meditation.

Our real attitudes toward others, what we think, say, and do concerning them, shows whether or not we really have fellowship with God. We can know God *only* in proportion to the fellowship we share with other people. Are we judging others by appearances? Do we have any hidden negative attitudes, such as prejudice or bigotry, that are blinding us? Are we unwilling to overlook others' mistakes? Are we unaware that a spark of God lives in everyone? If we answer "yes" to any of these questions, we are not living in true harmony with other people. Disharmony with others is the result of thinking that God is more in ourselves than in them, or that they have less divine power, love, and mercy than we do. When we are out of harmony with anyone, we are out of harmony with God, preventing us from experiencing true companionship with Him.

If we have any hard feelings toward anyone, we need to go within and pray, forgiving them the way God forgives us. No matter how we have been treated, we can love others for what they *really* are, not what they seem to be. We can love them because the Divine within them deserves our devotion.

Jesus showed us how to live in fellowship with God and man. He stayed in harmony with God through prayer and meditation; yet He didn't separate Himself from people: He lived among them, sharing their sorrows and relieving their suffering. He taught that love and service go together and dedicated His life to serving others. He loved others so much that He gave His life to overcome sin and death. He gave us only one commandment, ". . .love one another; even as I have loved you. . ." (John 13:34, RSV)

44

Our Need for Fellowship

Through the ages man has had an urgent need to understand himself and his relationship to others and to God. He has needed to realize that these relationships can't be separated, for they are really one. It isn't possible to separate God from His creations, for all souls are made in His likeness and He is expressing through them. (See Genesis 1:27.) When we realize that we are all one in Him, we know that we can't love God and hate another child of His. We realize that we must love not only our friends, but also our enemies (Luke 6:30-38; I John 4:20-21). When we truly understand our enemies and love them, we have an inner longing for them to know the way. We refuse to judge, hate, or seek revenge. We realize that the "terrible" things they do are really a misuse of the one power, the misdirection of the power of good. When we think this way, we can have a greater understanding for individuals, groups, and even nations. We as individuals must have "peace on earth, good will toward men" before whole nations can experience it. The millennium[1] is ours when love and brotherhood are built into the hearts of all men.

The first place to begin living brotherly love is at home. When our thoughts, words and actions show love, they have a beneficial effect on family members. Unkind words can hurt both the speaker and the person who receives them. If we feel upset, angry, or critical, we can refuse to let it show. By taking a moment to go within and pray, we can remember how and why we love the other person. Then we can replace our negative thoughts with positive ones and speak wisely.

Restoring Fellowship

Many of us keep saying that we want to know God, but do we really mean it? Are we willing to give up our selfish desires? Are we willing to love, forgive, and serve others? Some of us may complain that the way is too difficult, or that karmic debts hold us back. If we concentrate on or talk about our problems, we give them the strength to recur (Matthew 7:1, 2; Job 3:25).

Instead of listening to the doubting lower nature, we can believe the words of Jesus. He said, "Take my yoke upon you. . . my yoke is easy, and my burden light." (Matthew 11:29, 30, NCE) When we are united (yoked) in His fellowship, no burden is too hard to bear (I Corinthians 10:13). He said, "I am the vine, and you the branches. He who dwells in me, as I dwell in

---

1. "Millennium" means one thousand years of peace. See Revelation 20:4.

him, bears much fruit; for apart from me you can do nothing."
(John 15:5, NEB) He promised, "And I, when I am lifted up from
the earth, will draw all men to myself." (John 12:32, RSV)

Jesus lived and revealed ". . .the fellowship. . .which from the
beginning of the world hath been hid in God. . ." (Ephesians 3:9,
KJV) Let us share this revelation with others: G—O—O—D
N—E—W—S! Now it can be told—God is love; God is in each of
us. We are all one in Him. This is the gospel (good news) of Jesus
Christ! His love is restoring us to realization of at-one-ment with
God.

Conclusion

How have we treated others? According to the law of karma,
we can expect to be treated the same way. There is no reason to be
afraid if we have been following God's voice of divine grace and
love that is within us. If we haven't followed it in the past, we can
begin now by applying love through our thoughts, words, and
actions.

If we have a problem with someone, we can take the situation to
God through prayer and leave it with Him as we meditate. If we
have done all that we know to do and the problem continues to
seem unresolved, we can face it with the faith that, ". . .for those
who love God all things work together unto good. . ." (Romans
8:28, NCE) Through His loving mercy we are learning the lessons
which provide us with the opportunities to meet our karma
through His law of love—the grace of meeting our past debts by
forgiving, loving, and serving others.

"Great peace have they which love Thy law: and nothing shall
offend them." (Psalms 119:165, KJV) Regardless of what others
do, we can refuse to be offended; we can choose to live in
fellowship. We can do away with criticism or judging others when
we realize that every soul lives, moves, and has its being in Him;
each an equally important unit within the wholeness of God (Acts
17:28). With the awareness of this fellowship we live in peace, for
we know we are *all* one with Christ, and co-heirs to His promises:

"And be assured, I am with you always, to the end of time."
(Matthew 28:20, NEB)

"Set your troubled hearts at rest. Trust in God always; trust
also in me. There are many dwelling-places in my Father's
house. . . I am going there on purpose to prepare a place for you.
And. . .I shall come again and receive you to myself, so that where
I am you may be also. . ." (John 14:1-3, NEB)

"Peace I leave with you; my peace I give to you. . .Let not your hearts be troubled, neither let them be afraid." (John 14:27, RSV)

Growth Experiences

1. *Name Acrostics:* Choose a person's name. Print it *down* instead of across. Use capital letters:

           A   J
           L   O
           I   N
           C   E
           E   S

   Then choose a word that starts with each of the letters. Describe the person. Remember to choose words that show the person's good qualities. Seeing the good in others helps us to have fellowship.

Affectionate	Joyous
Loyal	Obedient
Incomparable	Neat
Classy	Enthusiastic
Earnest	Smiling

2. Design a symbol for fellowship. It might help you to analyze some club or organization symbols. Look in magazines for further ideas. For a good inspirational aid, see *Symbols and the Self*, by Violet M. Shelley, A.R.E. Press. Also, see the "Symbols Chart" on page 88 of this book.

3. Practice fellowship at home for one week. Choose one family member who needs your fellowship the most. List all his or her good points. Make a chart to show what *you* will do to bring about harmony. Put a check mark by each item on your list each time that you do it. At the end of the week, evaluate. Did the other person change? Did you change? Do you understand the other person better? Do you understand yourself better? Do you need to try this experiment for another week? With another person?

Study Group Activities

1. Do #1 above. Have everyone write his name on a piece of paper. Mix up the papers. Let everyone draw someone else's name and make up an acrostic analysis. After everyone has finished his acrostic, read them aloud and present them to the persons named. The acrostics could be done in felt-tipped pen, on star-shaped or flower-shaped pieces of construction

paper cut into four-inch squares. These may be used as name tags for the meetings or placed on bulletin boards.

2. Do #2 above. Discuss ideas and design a fellowship symbol for your group. Let each member copy it for his or her bulletin board.
3. Do #3 above. Have everyone compare experiences.

Lesson 7
PATIENCE

Bible Verse: "In your patience possess ye your souls." (Luke 21:19, KJV)

Prayer Affirmation: Creator and Giver of Life, just as Your presence in the earth is merciful and patient, guide us so we may express these same qualities as we face life's challenges. (Based on Edgar Cayce reading 262-24.)

Introduction

God is patient. His unending patience is reflected in everything He has created—from the stars and planets of the universe to the caves and valleys of the earth. His patience extends even to the souls of men, for He is willing to wait as long as it will take for all mankind to realize at-one-ment with Him (II Peter 3:9).

Some dictionaries define patience as calmly meeting suffering, obstacles, or delay without complaint. But the spiritual definition implies that patience is much more than calm endurance—it is the humility (selflessness) and purity of purpose that make us able to meet every challenge with loving thoughts, words, and actions. In other words, patience is expressing love. When we show real love to others, we do not impose our wills upon them, nor do we allow them to impose their wills upon us. Loving patience, then, isn't passive submission or being a "doormat"; it is a real spiritual force that rises to meet every challenge.

Patience is an activity of the God-mind of our soul. Although patience is one of a number of soul qualities, it is unique because it makes all the other soul qualities active in our lives. It takes patience to cooperate, know ourselves, follow our Ideal, express faith, and live in virtue, understanding, and fellowship.

The Value of Patience

The amount of patience we express indicates the level of our spiritual development. Our patience shows us whether we have

49

overcome past tests or been defeated by them. For example, let's look back for a moment to a particular problem we have faced in the past. Did we meet it patiently or impatiently? If we met it patiently, we had already learned (in this life or a previous one) the spiritual lesson involved. If we met it impatiently, we had not yet learned the lesson. Therefore, we can use patience as a measuring stick to discover the spiritual lessons that we still need to learn. Until we apply patience to whatever situations we find ourselves in, we will continue to meet similar difficulties.

When we discover the areas where we tend to be impatient, we shouldn't feel guilty, discouraged, or impatient with ourselves. What a hell we live in if we do! Instead, we should resolve to learn from our mistakes, and to face our problems with the attitude that they are opportunities to learn the lessons necessary for spiritual growth. God gives us the insights we need to meet and solve every problem and learn every lesson. He is *always* with us, guiding and helping us when we are willing to turn within and listen to His voice.

It takes patience to reach the Holy of Holies, the throne within, where we meet God. Over and over, we need to go within in prayer and meditation and seek His companionship and guidance. If we become impatient and lose our self-control, we can become fearful, shutting off our awareness of His presence. When we walk the path of loving patience, we truly will "possess our souls," find at-one-ment with God, and hear His voice of guidance.

Each time we patiently face and conquer a difficulty, we strengthen and beautify our souls (I Corinthians 3:12-14). Just as an oyster forms a pearl from patiently meeting an irritation, so may we form within our souls a spiritual pearl of great value when we patiently meet every problem (Matthew 13:45, 46).

How Do We Become Patient?

Acquiring patience is actually the process of giving up our own selfishness. This requires a constant prayerful attitude of self-inspection. How are we meeting our daily problems? Are we critical or resentful? What are we saying and doing to others? Are we avoiding quick, angry responses that could hurt them? Are we really living our Ideal? We must live in perfect harmony with our Ideal if we want to possess patience. The real secret of "unselfing" ourselves is to become so centered in God that we forget ourselves, think of others first, and then begin to serve them.

We need to realize that becoming patient is a step-by-step process. It doesn't happen overnight. Daily, we should do the best we know with what we have, right where we are. That is all that is expected of us. As we live what we know, the spirit guides us and we come closer and closer to living our Ideal.

As we seek to express patience, our souls bring into our experience the tests or trials that can help us learn this important lesson (Hebrews 12:6). The Bible says, "My brothers, you will always have your trials but, when they come, try to treat them as a happy privilege; you understand that your faith is only put to the test to make you patient, but patience too is to have its practical results so that you will become fully developed, complete, with nothing missing." (James 1:2-4, JB) The selfish lower nature must be cleansed and purified. We must sacrifice it in the purifying fire of divine love if we want to live in at-one-ment with God. When the tests come, we need to realize that the influences of the inner spirit are stronger than the outer circumstances. We need to turn within and listen for the guidance of the Comforter, the Holy Spirit (Matthew 10:19, 20). When we follow this guidance, each trying experience will become an opportunity to find an even closer attunement with God. His Spirit will give us the strength and patience to overcome the selfish lower nature.

The lessons we learn through patience not only help us to grow, but can aid others, too. They may want to follow the example we have set and exercise the patience that is necessary for them to solve their problems. As we express God's love and help others to find it, we grow even closer to Him ourselves.

Let's begin now, through faith and patience, to live what we have already learned. If we refuse to apply what we know and give in to the desires of the lower nature, we simply delay the tests and their resulting growth opportunities that can lead us to a closer attunement with God. Now, just for today, let's live the way we would live if Jesus walked beside us.

Conclusion

Patience is the basic building block for soul development. The Cayce readings indicate that patience is not only a soul quality but part of the third dimension, along with time and space. The function of time is to help us understand our ideas. Space is the vehicle that allows us to inspect the ideas that we have brought into material existence. But it is through patience that we discover our motives, the purposes behind our actualized ideas. Through patience we determine whether or not our ideas are loving and in harmony with our Ideal. Thus, patience allows us to measure not only our weaknesses but our strengths, and to see the possibility of developing even greater strengths through expressing our soul qualities.

The patience shown in our lives indicates whether we have overcome our past tests or been defeated by them. It is the true measure of the maturity of our spiritual development, for the patience we manifest, more than any other soul quality, shows what we are now, have been, and what we really want to be. Our ability to express patience shows whether we can overlook the faults and misconceptions of others, or if we think that *our* ways and beliefs are the only ones that are valid. If we feel impatient, we need to examine ourselves to see if our own opinions are so important that we would be willing to indulge in an ego trip which might cause us to lose our awareness of God. Isn't loss of God Consciousness a high price to pay for pride and unforgiveness? (See Mark 8:34-37.)

If we condemn other people's shortcomings or differences, we are actually saying that we can't forgive them their "wrong" ideas. The Master Jesus was asked, " 'Lord, how often am I to forgive my brother if he goes on wronging me? As many as seven times?' Jesus replied, 'I do not say seven times; I say seventy times seven.' " (Matthew 18:21-22, NEB) Are we patiently willing to show such unending forgiveness, or do we prefer to get even with those who "cross" us? The first attitude is one of love and grace; the second causes us to live in the misery of our lower natures—a self-made "hell." When we are impatient, we receive impatience in return (karmic law). But when we patiently live what we know, we grow in grace, wisdom, and understanding. Let our prayer be, "Lord, with Your help I shall show the patience of the Christ." Then let us not only try to be patient with others, but let us serve them. As we do, we become more aware of God's presence within us, which in turn enables us to become even more patient. Also, as we serve others, we are helping to bring about the coming of the Lord. When can He come? Now! For even today His presence can live and express in the earth through us as we show patience to others and serve them. (See Matthew 25:40-45.)

Growth Experiences

1. Recall a problem you have had with someone. What did you think? What did you say and do? Replay the scene in your mind, but this time think, say, and act with loving patience as you imagine the scene. Write down the new scene you created. How did the other person act in the new scene? Next time a similar incident occurs, try to "play the scene" with the loving

patience you practiced in your imagination. You can apply this method to any recurring problem.

2. One way to apply patience is to *really* clean your room or your home. Clean out the closet and the drawers. Discard useless objects. Any usable things you don't need could be donated to Goodwill, the Salvation Army, or some other charity. While you are cleaning your premises, clean out your "mental closets," too. Let go of negative mental habits. As you let go of any resentments, hostilities, fears, etc., get rid of any material objects that remind you of unpleasant memories. Don't cling to the past. Live in the beauty of the present!

3. A service project: Look through a magazine and find a large picture that appeals to you. Cut it out and mount it with rubber cement to a piece of cardboard or an old file folder. Cut off any uneven edges. Now use a felt-tipped pen to make a jigsaw puzzle. Cut it out and place the pieces in a large envelope or box. Give the puzzle to a hospital's children's ward, to a retirement home, or to a child, friend, or shut-in.

Study Group Activities

1. Do #1 above. Compare experiences. Members may act out some of the new scenes.
2. Do #2 above. Share insights with the group. Have the members contribute their leftover articles to charity. Plan a field trip to donate the articles.
3. Do #3 above. Have each member make two puzzles, one to share with another member. Shuffle the envelopes, then let each member choose one to work and keep. Give the extra puzzles away.

Lesson 8
THE OPEN DOOR

Bible Verse: "Behold, I stand at the door, and knock; if any man hear my voice, and open the door, I will come in to him, and will sup with him, and he with me." (Revelation 3:20, KJV)

Prayer Affirmation: Father, through the Christ Spirit, the door to the heavenly Kingdom, may I know You as You know me. Show me the way! (Based on Edgar Cayce reading 262-27.)

> Why do you hesitate, my soul?
> Don't you know that new strength comes
>   only by renewing your faith
> Again and again, and by constant effort?
> And can you even hope to catch
> The slightest glimpse of God
> If you fail to offer fully
> The helping hand which opens the door?

Introduction

Every soul's eternal destiny is the Kingdom of God—the realization and expression of our at-one-ment with the Infinite. No matter who or where we are in the complex scheme of creation, we have an inner desire to reach this goal. If we fail to understand our inner longing, we may hunger to fulfill it by satisfying the selfish desires of the lower nature. If we give in to the lower nature, then we struggle against the unchangeable laws of an all-wise Creator. Eventually we all have to make God's will our own, stop struggling against His laws, and move with them. When we do, we find the heavenly Kingdom and gain peace through the realization that, "I and my Father are one." (John 10:30, KJV)

Jesus Christ became the way, the open door, to reveal to us the pattern for reaching the heavenly Kingdom. He said, "...I am the way, and the truth, and the life." (John 14:6, NCE) "Behold, I stand at the door and knock; if any man hear my voice, and open

54

the door, I will come in to him, and will sup (commune) with him, and he with me." (Revelation 3:20, KJV; authors' parentheses) How do we open the door? We begin to open it as we seek to let the Christ Consciousness, the Holy Spirit, express in our lives. The Christ Consciousness is the awareness we have in our souls that we are one with God. This awareness is printed in pattern deep within the mind, waiting to be awakened by the will. As we seek to make our wills work in harmony with God's will, the Christ Consciousness begins to be revealed in our lives. Then *we* become doors that open for the full expression of His Spirit in the earth. The more we act as doors for God to express *in* and through us to others, the more we open our inner doors to the Kingdom (Luke 17:21).

The previous lessons have emphasized the soul qualities we must express to open wide our spiritual doors. Have we really been living these lessons? Do we really cooperate? Do we know who we are and how we relate to others? Is our Ideal truly God-centered? What about our faith? Are we living the fruits of the spirit? (See Galatians 5:22-24.) Are we really patient? We need to *live* these lessons to make active in our lives the soul qualities that open the door to the heavenly Kingdom.

Selfish Thoughts Close the Door

If the door to the inner Kingdom is shut, it has been closed by our own selfish thoughts. We need to realize that although the spirit gives us life, the *mind* shapes the physical existence. To illustrate: Think of a piece of clay as the spiritual substance of life. Imagine the mind as the sculptor planning to shape the clay into a design. Finally, the sculptor (the mind) directs the physical shaping of the clay (the life) and creates the finished product (the physical condition).

Since our minds mold, shape, and direct our lives, our thoughts are important. Selfish thoughts keep us so focused on ourselves that we can't be aware of God. If we concentrate on negative thoughts—self-condemnation, doubt, lack, hurt, fear, resentment, etc.—we shut so tightly our inner doors to the God Consciousness that eventually not even a trace of His light can shine through to our awareness. By our own choice, we have closed the door on the heavenly light and are imprisoned in the darkness, the hell, of our own negative thinking. Habitual negative thought patterns can create depression, despair, or illness; they can even result in suicides, murders, or other crimes. (See Galatians 5:19-21.)

When we live in a pattern of self-centeredness, we eventually come to feel that life has cheated us. We shut out others and we cease to give to them or to help them. The door to the Kingdom swings two ways. As we open the inner door to God, it also swings open to others. If we close the door to others, we close the inner door to God's Kingdom, keeping His guidance and abundance from manifesting in our own lives.

Opening the Door

We open the door to the Kingdom through faith, service, and love. Faith lights the way by banishing our fears; service is the doorstep that invites us through. Love leads us past the selfishness that bars the door to awareness of God's inner abiding presence. Once the door is open, we commune with Him. His Holy Spirit guides, teaches, and helps us to remember all things (John 14:26).

To put faith, service, and love into action, we first must believe that God *is* and seek Him. Then we need to center our purpose, our Ideal, in Him and refuse to concentrate on any negative attitudes. Next we must surrender our wills to Him, dissolving our selfishness in the light of His love. When we have put aside our egos, the voice of the Christ Spirit guides us to a life of loving service.

Why should we serve others? A portion of the revelation that Christ Jesus came to share with us was that although each of us is unique, we are all part of the wholeness of God. Since we are so vitally linked together with one another and with God, we *are* our brothers' keepers. Jesus said, " '. . .when was it that we saw you hungry and fed you, or thirsty and gave you drink, a stranger and took you home, or naked and clothed you? When did we see you ill or in prison, and come to visit you?' . . .'I tell you this: anything you did for one of my brothers here, however humble, you did for me.' " (See Matthew 25:38-40, NEB.)

A smile, an encouraging word, a kind favor, can uplift those around us. Spirituality must be shared with others in a material way because we live in a three-dimensional world. Can we really help others find the way of oneness with God if we think and talk about brotherly love but fail to live it? When we apply the simple acts of love, opportunities come for us to show even deeper evidences of God's light working through our lives. The more we manifest the Christ Consciousness, the more we become living examples of God's love—open doors of help to others, doers of the word and not hearers only (James 1:22).

The first and main reason for serving others is to help them find the Light, the Christ. However, we benefit too. Just as a gushing current purifies a stagnant pool, we are purified when we let God's Holy Spirit flow through us to bless and serve others.

Conclusion

Many spend lifetimes seeking to gain an earthly kingdom. To possess one is a responsibility and an honor. It gives a person a feeling of accomplishment. But it is so much greater to possess the Kingdom of the Father, prepared for us from the foundation of the world (Matthew 25:34). Only our selfishness can prevent us from having this Kingdom. When we are willing to sacrifice our selfishness and replace it with love, the spirit can lead us to the Christ Kingdom, where we receive our birthright: ". . .he who believes in me will also do the works that I do; and greater works than these will he do, because I go to the Father. Whatever you ask in my name, I will do it, that the Father may be glorified in the Son. . ." (John 14:12-13, RSV) "All power is given unto me in heaven and in earth." (Matthew 28:18, KJV) When we seek, we will be shown the way, for we are heirs and co-heirs with Christ Jesus to the Kingdom of Heaven (Romans 8:17).

As we seek to follow the Christ path, we need to realize that through God's law we are judged by the way we deal with others. As we give, we receive; measure for measure is returned to us. As we lift others, we are lifted. As we forgive, we are forgiven; not because God wills it, but because *we* have made the choice by our own words and actions (Matthew 7:1-2). God's loving-kindness wants all of us to experience the Kingdom, but He has laws that are just, and we must cooperate with them if we are to know Him. Since God's law of grace is love, we attain the Kingdom only as we reach out in love and sympathy to those who need our aid (Romans 13:10). We must be willing to help their needs at the level of their understanding, realizing that each person is right where he needs to be for his own development, whatever his circumstances.

The door to the inner Kingdom opens, and we know God as we become living examples of His qualities. We don't reach this stage all at once. We reach a higher consciousness through the patient effort of applying daily what we already know. Little by little, line by line, precept upon precept, we come closer to awareness of the Christ Consciousness as we let His Spirit express in our lives. Even though we may have trials, we are able to meet them, for we can draw on the Christ's force, power, and activity. He has promised, "Lo, I am with you alway, even unto the end of the world." (Matthew 28:20, KJV)

Growth Experiences

1. What kind of pattern would you make to symbolize the door to the Christ Consciousness? Would it be like a dress pattern? a blueprint? a road map? a raised-print type? What would the sides look like? What would its dimensions be? What directions would you put on it?

    Make a pattern to represent the Christ Consciousness. Use whatever materials are necessary to complete your project. Refer to the "Symbols Chart," page 88, for helpful hints.

2. Word find:

```
A N C O O P E R A T I O N T E N K
R A O P V I M A R R E O E A C L N
E C N E I T A P E O I Z V G O M O
W R E N G O N M Y T W O O F F C W
V O N D E P L E A N D V L A D A S
I S E O T D O T R Y D A I L Y N E
R S S O B H I S P R E S E N C E L
G A S R U D O D E D I T A T I O F
I N A A E D G A I N E I T A P A R
N D N M U N D E R S T A N D I N G
I C D B T A H L E E R B U T T E R
A R B I R T L D A W I L H N O P U
B O R P I H S W O L L E F R O A M
E W E R V E T D R I L S R U S T M
A N D O E M B O I L Y S O P L A Y
```

    Circle the words from the list below as you find them in the puzzle above. You may move across, down, backwards, and diagonally. See if you can find two other words related to the material in this book. Also, find any extra unrelated words, just for fun.

PRAYER	FAITH	OPEN DOOR
MEDITATION	VIRTUE	HIS PRESENCE
COOPERATION	UNDERSTANDING	CROSS AND CROWN
KNOW SELF	FELLOWSHIP	ONENESS
THE IDEAL	PATIENCE	LOVE

3. Buy clay or make your own from the following recipe: Mix equal portions of flour and salt; gradually add enough water to make dough pliable. Knead until dough is clay consistency. It is good to use all of this preparation when it is made. It can mildew if stored too long in plastic bags.

Make a clay sculpture. Can you make a good sculpture without planning it? If you have no particular shape as a goal, what kind of sculpture "happens"? Try it and see. Next, plan a design for a sculpture. Use a picture or a photo as a pattern; close your eyes and "see" each step you need to take in forming your sculpture. Visualize the finished product. Now, sculpt your design. Compare your two efforts. Why is the mind important? How do thoughts shape our lives? Can any physical action be performed without the help of our minds (conscious, subconscious, or superconscious)?

Study Group Activities

1. Do #1 above. Compare and discuss efforts. Share insights. Place your patterns on bulletin boards.
2. The group members can do #2 above, starting at the same time. See who finishes first. Who found the most "unlisted" words?
3. The group can do #3 above as a cooperative project. Two or three can work together on one art object. The first object can be unplanned by the group. Have each person add shapes without consulting the other members. The second object can be planned and discussed by the group. Then the members can cooperatively form the second sculpture. Allow a certain time for each effort. Afterwards allot a certain time period for each group to share their object with the other groups and compare experiences. If the study group is small, let everyone work as one group on the two endeavors. Does cooperation make a difference? Does having a pattern in mind help?

Lesson 9
IN HIS PRESENCE

Bible Verse: "I will be ever present in your midst: I will be your God, and you shall be My people." (Leviticus 26:12, *Torah*)

Prayer Affirmation: Heavenly Father, express Your Kingdom in the earth through me. Daily may the light of Your word shine through me to others. May others see Your presence in my actions, and glorify You. May I glorify You by seeing Your presence in others. (Based on Cayce reading 262-30; see also Matthew 5:16.)

Introduction

"Lift up your heads, you gates,
lift yourselves up, you everlasting doors,
that the king of glory may come in."

(Psalms 24:7, NEB)

The way we look at life depends on our concepts of God. Our thoughts, words, and actions are based on our viewpoints of Him. The ideal we have in life and our inner and outer experiences reflect the kind of "god" we really worship.

Who or what is God, then? God is the Spirit in everyone and every thing, here and in every plane of existence. All creations are heading toward the awareness that this Spirit is One. "Hear, O Israel, the Lord our God is one. . ." (Deuteronomy 6:4; Mark 12:29, KJV)

People describe the Oneness with many different names—Jehovah, Yah, Yahweh, Allah, Dios, Dio, Dieu, Gott, etc. Others may call God Great Spirit, Creative Energy, Divine Intelligence, Infinite Wisdom, Mother-Father God, and so on. No matter what we call Him, God is One.

God cannot be separated from His creations. If we think that there is more than one power, that God is found only outside us,

60

or that God is not in everyone, we suffer from a belief called "duality."

In Western religious thought duality is often represented by a belief in another power called "Lucifer," "Satan," or the "devil." Redefining these terms may help clarify these concepts.[1] "Lucifer" means "light-bringer" in Latin, "morning star" in Hebrew, and the planet "Venus" in English (Isaiah 14:12, KJV). "Lucifer" could be viewed as that spiritual portion of ourselves that is perfect until selfishness enters in and we "fall," or separate our consciousness from the awareness of God.

"Satan" in Hebrew means "enemy" or "adversary." Satan might therefore stand for the inner enemy—our own selfish thoughts and desires.

"Devil" means "slanderer," "liar," or "deceiver." This term could refer to the confusion we experience and reflect when our selfishness manifests in the physical realm. Selfishness confines us to the physical consciousness and the information we receive through the senses. The senses deceive us, allowing us to perceive only a fragment of reality.

At the conscious level, man tends to sort out his sensory perceptions and label them "good" or "bad." Limiting ourselves to this awareness could be termed "eating of the tree of the knowledge of good and evil"—duality. According to the Biblical story (Genesis 2, 3), this is what is called the "fall," the banishment of man from the Garden of Eden, where the "tree of life" grew. When we live in the awareness of the oneness, the superconscious mind, we are "eating of the tree of life."[2] The "flaming, two-edged sword" that bars us from the "tree of life" might represent the subconscious, which keeps us from the unlimited power of the superconscious until we are loving and unselfish.

When we believe in duality, we can view the "devil" as the cause of our troubles, the scapegoat for our own selfishness. Also, we can view others as followers of this "other power" and feel justified in hating, persecuting, and even killing them. It is easy to see that the duality concept can create fear, confusion, disharmony, murders, and wars—the direct opposites to the fruits of the spirit of love (Galatians 5:19-22).

Following is a chart to illustrate further the concept of oneness versus duality:

---

1. References: *Webster's Dictionary* and *Strong's Exhaustive Concordance of the Bible.*
2. Revelation 2:7, KJV—"To him that overcometh will I give to eat of the tree of life, which is in the midst of the paradise of God."

The Concept of Oneness Versus
the Concept of Duality

Oneness
If we are unselfish, loving, united in consciousness with God, we see life through a viewpoint of light, of oneness: God's energy expressing as Holy Spirit, Son, and Father through all levels of self and creation. "To the pure all things are pure." (Titus 1:15, RSV)

Duality
If we are selfish, unloving, limited in awareness of God, we see life through a viewpoint of darkness, of duality: God's energy in conflict with another power expressing as "Lucifer," "Satan," or the "devil," bringing forth both good and evil through all levels of self and creation. "God is light, and in him is no darkness at all." (I John 1:5, KJV)

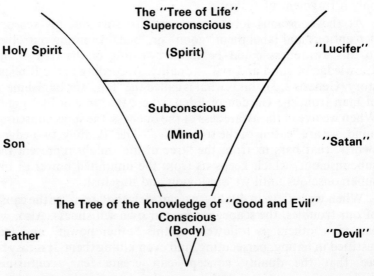

Cayce reading 2771-1 states: "Each soul—as it manifests in the earth—is body, mind and spirit; just as there is in the Godhead the God the father, God the mind, God the holy spirit. These—as Father, Son and Holy Ghost—are one. These terms of expression are used in this three-dimensional world."

The only anti-Christ (anti-Love), "Satan," or "devil" we ever have to face is our own selfishness, which creates a sense of

separation from God through our misuse of His power within us.
God is all-powerful (omnipotent), all-knowing (omniscient), and present everywhere and in everything (omnipresent). In other words, "Christ is all, and in all." (Colossians 3:11, RSV) When we realize this, we can change our lives. We can start living in harmony with the laws of the Oneness—love, forgiveness, and service.

How to Know God's Presence

Since God is One, and we live and move and have our being in Him (Acts 17:28), we are *always* in His presence. To be aware of Him, we only need to stop, meditate, and listen for His still, small voice. Although He is not a person, He can be very personal to us. Even though He is God to everyone, our personal relationship with Him can make us want to call Him "Father," for we are all His children.

During His earthly life Jesus stressed oneness with the Father. He stated that He Himself could do nothing; the Father within Him did everything (John 14:10, 11). We, too, can begin to do what Jesus did when we experience the oneness—commune with God's presence within us (John 14:12, 13).

A part of us is always aware of God's presence—the Christ Consciousness or superconsciousness (Matthew 18:10). His spirit of truth, then, is always within us and guides us. If we are unaware of this presence, it is because of our selfish concentration on our "own" powers and mental abilities.

To cultivate the attitudes that lead to awareness of our atonement with Him, the following suggestions may help:

1. We need to believe that God is, that He is good, and that His will for us is good. (See Psalms 100:5; James 1:17.)

2. We need to realize that God is with us now and always, and gives us the wisdom to know Him. "If any of you falls short in wisdom, he should ask God for it and it will be given him, for God is a generous giver who neither refuses nor reproaches anyone. But he must ask in faith, without a doubt in his mind. . ." (James 1:5-6, NEB)

3. It is important to submit our wills to God. We need to be willing to follow His rules, not ours. Jesus said, "If ye love me, keep my commandments." (John 14:15, KJV) ". . .you shall love the Lord your God with all your heart, and with all your soul, and with all your mind, and with all your strength. . .you shall love your neighbor as yourself." (Mark 12:30-31, RSV)

4. We need to set aside a time for prayer and meditation and consistently seek to communicate with God, making sure that our Ideal is in Him. (See Psalms 19:14.)
5. We should view everyone and everything through God's eye of love. We need to realize that everyone is expressing his attitude toward God at his own level of understanding. No matter how another person may act, God is in that person and loves him. Criticism and condemnation of others prevent us from realizing at-one-ment with God.
6. We need to observe the laws of clean living, maintaining balance at all three levels of being; for we are constantly reflecting our understanding of God's presence physically, mentally, spiritually.
   a. A healthy body shows that we are observing physical laws of diet, exercise, and rest. Even the smallest details that involve taking care of the body are important. Either we are in spiritual, mental, and physical harmony with the laws of good health, or we are in disharmony with them and express dis-ease.
   b. Just as physical activities reflect the body's stamina, mental activities reflect the strength of the mind. We have man-made laws and customs that partially govern and control our physical actions, but the problem of thought-control is a personal one. We need to realize that our minds are creating our circumstances. We must learn to control and guide our thoughts, centering them in God's law of love.
   c. How spiritual are our lives? Others are looking at us for signs of spirituality; they are influenced by what they see. Our surroundings, our friends, and our activities show others how near we are to living God's law of love.

Experiencing God's Presence

As we lay aside self-interest and place our faith and trust in the inner voice of God's word, each of us will experience His living presence. As we submit our wills to His divine guidance, we are led step by step to know Him. We find peace. His Spirit communicates with us and leads us to a better understanding of ourselves, our brothers, our friends, and our enemies. His presence surrounds us and His light shines ahead to guide us. He keeps us from stumbling. He keeps us from all harm. He leads us to serve others joyously. Let us live *every* moment in the awareness of His presence.

64

"Come! Let my heart be lifted in praise and adoration of the wondrous love that the Father sheds upon the children of men. Come, let all be glad in the opportunities that are given to serve in His name day by day. Come, let us be joyous in the truth that, 'Inasmuch as ye did it unto the least of these my little ones, ye did it unto me.' [Matthew 25:40, KJV] Let the love of the Son be magnified in our lives that others may know that the joyousness of service brings peace and harmony to our hearts as we serve. Come! Give thanks unto Him, for we would make our lives, our own bodies, a dwelling place of the love that the Father would manifest unto His children. Come, give place to His holy name, that there may come joyousness in the hearts of men at the coming of the Christ into the lives and the experiences of many." (Cayce reading 281-14)

Individual Growth Experiences

1. Using the poetic form below, write two or more cinquains showing that you recognize the presence of God in at least two other people. Challenge: Write one of the poems about a person you find difficult to deal with. Be sure to keep the poem positive.

	Cinquain Form
Noun	*David*
Two adjectives	*Diligent, intelligent*
Three verbs	*Writing, reading, lecturing*
Summary statement	*A source of help to others*
Repeat noun or use a synonym	*Advisor*

2. Do you always use the same name for God? Choose several different names for God. Use a new one each time you pray. See if you feel comfortable using various names as introductions to prayer. Which name do you like best? (For more names for God, see an encyclopedia.)

Group Activities

1. Do #1 above. Use group members as subjects, each one choosing another to write about. Share the poems with each other and let each one take the poem about himself home for posting on his bulletin board. (Homework challenge: Each member write a cinquain about a person he finds difficult. Let him post it on his bulletin board to remind him of the beauty in that person.)

2. Review the numbered suggestions in this chapter (pages 63-64) for cultivating attudes that lead to awareness of at-one-ment. Write a group affirmation using these ideas. Example: "God exists. He is Love, and wants only good things for all His children. God is with us now. . ." If possible, type the affirmations and make copies so that each member can have one. Or let each member copy the completed group effort. Or use butcher or shelf paper plus felt-tipped pens in various colors to write the affirmation, and make a large copy to be posted at future meetings. Roll up the paper between meetings.

Individual sentences of the total affirmation might be put on construction paper and used as bookmarks. Decorations might make them special.

Copies of the completed affirmation or favorite single sentences of it can be posted on the members' bulletin boards.

Lesson 10

THE CROSS
AND THE CROWN

Bible Verse: "Fear none of those things which thou shalt suffer. . . Be thou faithful unto death, and I will give thee a crown of life." (Revelation 2:10, KJV)

Prayer Affirmation: Our Father-God, may we understand what Jesus overcame through the cross and what glory lies ahead through the crown. May the blessings You promised through Him be with us, as we study together in His name. (Based on Edgar Cayce reading 262-34.)

> ". . .Jesus said, 'If you dwell within the revelation I have brought, you are indeed my disciples; you shall know the truth, and the truth will set you free.' " (John 8:31-32, NEB)

Introduction

For some time now we have tried to apply the truths that Jesus Christ taught and lived. It is to be hoped that we have built some of them into our consciousness. But have we really made the *big* decision? Are we truly ready to follow the Christ path of complete unselfishness—the Way of the Cross?

At this point we need to ask some questions and search for some plausible answers. How did the Way of the Cross begin? Why did Jesus have to bear the cross? Do we have to do the same thing? What are the meanings of the cross and the crown for today?

How the Way of the Cross Began

In the vibrating, eternal cosmos of God, the essence of all that is has always existed. There has always been only one essence, one God; and all that is has been made up of It. God chose to express His infinite essence by individualizing Himself into many differing vibrational frequencies within His wholeness (Genesis

1).[1] We might compare this individualizing process with a symphony composed of different musical notes, playing in harmony with each other. Divine thought could change the "melody" by varying the sequence of the vibrational frequencies of each "note." Those of us now on earth were among the spiritual children, "notes," "lights," or "stars" of His being, whose vibrations harmoniously contributed to the divine symphony. The Bible refers to this occasion as the time when "...the morning stars sang together, and all the sons of God shouted for joy." (Job 38:7, KJV)

Each soul participating in God's symphony was created with spirit, mind, and free will—triune units reflecting the triune God. With free will, each soul could choose to work in harmony with God's wholeness or to create discordant melodies of its own. Some decided to exert their free wills and live inharmoniously, selfishly. When the decision was made to go against, or to "cross," the will of the divine Creator, the time of the cross began. (This is known as "the fall.")

Many souls continued to "cross" God in the beginning of the world, the three-dimensional plane of existence. Some wanted to manipulate His law to satisfy themselves in lower vibrational forms. Others opposed His law and misused the power given to them. Through sin, or selfishness, they entered materiality and slowly lost the awareness that they were one with God, each other, and everything in creation. They became trapped in the confusion of their own creative thought forms and the illusions of the senses. After a time, they even forgot that they were subject to the law of cause and effect, or karma. Selfish thoughts and desires triggered negative karma, creating problems, or crosses. Since the law of karma requires that created problems be met until they are overcome, souls were trapped in the earth in a self-created darkness of suffering and despair. Many were so enmeshed in materiality that they didn't remember who they were, why they existed, or where they should be going. Truly mankind was "lost" and needed to be shown the way to regain at-one-ment.[2]

Why Jesus Chose the Way of the Cross

Amilius, who later expressed as Jesus the Christ, was the

1. Genesis 1:26-28 tells of the individualization of the souls of mankind, spiritual emanations of God, pre-physical androgynous beings whose male-female properties were in perfect balance.
2. For detailed information on the creation and fall of man, read the "Philosophy Section" of *There Is a River*, by Thomas Sugrue, Dell Publishing Company, Inc., New York; and the *Trilogy on Creation*, by Eula Allen, A.R.E. Press, Virginia Beach, Virginia.

individualized spiritual expression of God through which all earthly creations came into being. He was aware of the plight of the souls as they became trapped in materiality through their selfishness. He knew that their sleeping spiritual essence had to be reawakened to Divine Awareness.

Therefore, He chose to express in a physical body to show the trapped souls a way to overcome the world. When He entered materiality He became known as Adam (Genesis 2).[3] He entered the realm of death, loss of awareness of at-one-ment, to reawaken the divine Awareness of those souls who had trapped themselves in thought forms of every description.

He chose to express in a superior physical form that would provide a pattern for improved physical incarnations of the thought forms. In doing so, He brought in physical death as well. Through death man could return to earth in different bodies to meet his selfishness through different experiences, until finally he could rid himself of selfish karma and realize oneness. Reincarnation or rebirth would give man unlimited occasions to meet and overcome, or "crucify," the selfishness that had caused his problems. Each earthly lifetime would provide repeated opportunities to realize and express at-one-ment, the "crown of life." (Revelation 2:10)

Step by step the Christ-soul (first called Amilius, then Adam) would re-enter materiality to help awaken mankind. (See John 1:1-14.) He had to experience all of man's trials—suffering, doubts, fears, weaknesses, temptations, etc., and overcome them all (Hebrews 2:18; Luke 22:37; Isaiah 53:5). "And he, Son though he was, learned obedience from the things that He suffered." (Hebrews 5:8, NCE) In other words, He had to overcome *self!* In totally conquering the physical lower nature with its temptations to glorify self, He, as Jesus, became the One who would lead all souls into harmony with their Source (Luke 4:1-13; John 12:32). Through love, not force or demand, Jesus would lead the souls to understand the truth of their being. (See Cayce reading 262-144.)

In the beginning of the world all things were given into the care of Amilius (Adam). Everything in the earth came under His command (Genesis 1:26). He was told to subdue the earth—which included the elements of the lower nature as well as materiality (Genesis 1:28; 2:19-20). Then, expressing as Jesus, He lived the Way of the Cross, finally conquering the earth nature. His

---

3. Genesis 2 is an account of the physical creation of man. At that time the souls began expressing in either male *or* female bodily forms.

salvation,[4] His path, is the crucifixion, the complete sacrifice of selfishness through love and service.

Thus, the first Adam brought in death; but the last Adam, Jesus, overcame it. His life, death, and resurrection show man the way to realize his divinity (John 10:34, 35), the eternal nature of his life, and the unity of all things. There is no death. "Death is swallowed up in victory," for Christ lives! (I Corinthians 15:22-50, 54, JB) He helps mankind even today.

We, Too, Must Bear a Cross

Some people believe that only Jesus needed to suffer a crucifixion. They feel that His cross experience took care of the sins of mankind, and that man's only obligation to God is to "believe in Jesus," without having to do anything himself. But "believing in Jesus" includes *following* His teachings and *living* His commandments, ". . .love one another, as I have loved you." (John 15:12, NEB) To live love we must crucify self, the ego, the selfish lower nature. Jesus said, "If any one wishes to be a follower of mine, he must leave self behind; he must take up his cross and come with me." (Matthew 16:24, NEB) "And whoever does not take up his cross and follow me is not worthy of me." (Matthew 10:38-39, LB)

The cross each of us must bear is for our own form of selfishness, whatever it may be. Selfishness takes many forms. A Biblical list includes: ". . .fornication, impurity, and indecency; idolatry and sorcery; quarrels, a contentious temper, envy, fits of rage, selfish ambitions, dissensions, party intrigues, and jealousies; drinking bouts, orgies, and the like." (Galatians 5:20, NEB) Selfishness can lead to criticism, gossip, hatred, resentment, or persecution of others. It can cause worry, doubt, or fear. It leads some people to worship power, fame, riches, self-glory, or honor. The Bible says, ". . .those who belong to Christ Jesus have crucified the lower nature with its passions and desires." (Galatians 5:24, NEB) To crucify our lower natures we must voluntarily give up our selfish egos through living mercy, forgiveness, and love—the path of the Master, the Way of the Cross. As we make our wills one with divine will, we reach the crown of glory and life—perfect attunement with God so that He can perfectly express through our lives.

To face our crosses and overcome them through love, we need the strength and power of Christ's help. When we are yoked

---

4. "Salvation" translated from Hebrew and Greek means aid, victory, prosperity, health help; to open, to free.

united, in harmony with Him, His presence aids us (Matthew 11:29-30). He can ease our burdens because He has faced *all* the trials and problems of the world and overcome them (John 16:33). All that *we* have to overcome are the trials we have created for ourselves, and we can do so with His help.

Christ's presence provides a reserve of power that makes us able to face our crosses, complete our purpose, and wear the crown. His Spirit leads us from sorrow, turmoil, hate, and weakness to joy, peace, love, and strength. Yoked with Him, we find that our burdens are truly light. Our happiness increases as we become more like Him, who became the Lord of lords and King of kings by way of the cross (Revelation 17:14).

He will lead us to realize our oneness with God, even as He realized His. Also, we will be able to *do* what He did. Jesus said, "Truly, truly, I say to you, he who believes in me will also do the works that I do; and greater works than these will he do, because I go to the Father." (John 14:12, RSV)

As we follow the Christ's example and daily meet and overcome our own crosses, we discover that we really want to help other people. Joyfully we help them with their crosses, or problems. Through loving service we complete our sacrifice of selfishness and become more and more at one with Him. As we help others bear their crosses, we fulfill many opportunities to show our gratitude to Jesus Christ, who made our way of escape from selfishness possible (I Corinthians 10:13).

The Meaning of the Cross and the Crown

The cross has several levels of symbolism. It symbolizes the shame of man's "fall," his opposition to God's law, and the resulting lowered consciousness. Personally, or individually, it stands for what each of us must overcome in our own lives—the crucifixion of our *own* forms of selfishness.

Since Christ Jesus overcame materiality, the cross has a deeper meaning for those who follow Him. It no longer stands for the shame of the fall, but for the glory of His overcoming the limitations of this physical plane. It is a symbol of the path by which *all* men can find the crown of at-one-ment even while in flesh: humility, instead of stubbornness; patience, not impulsiveness; faith, rather than fear; forgiveness, instead of holding grudges; and loving enemies, not hating them. When we live the Way of the Cross—selflessness, love, and service—we will realize the crown of our true Sonship (Romans 8:16, 17, 29).

71

Conclusion

After considering the difficulties of the cross, some of us might decide to follow our own path instead of the Way of the Cross. But *can* we give up? If we do, we will continue to live in the suffering caused by our own selfishness. We can't escape God or His law. God is everywhere. Sooner or later we will want to know and fulfill His purpose for our lives.

The purpose of life is to know ourselves, to be ourselves, yet one with God—His companions and expressions of His love to His creation. (See Cayce readings 3508-1 and 5749-14.) To accomplish our purpose, in faith we must "keep on keeping on" in the Christ path. When we try to follow Him, we may suffer persecution, for other people may not understand our beliefs and ideals (John 15:18-20; Matthew 5:10-12). They may even think that we are "evil," or "of the devil." (Matthew 10:24-25) Whatever the problem, as we continue to love even those who misunderstand us, God's power will adjust each situation, for ". . . all things work together for good to them that love God . . . " (Romans 8:28, KJV)

As we meet our crosses and overcome each temptation, we know we are heirs and joint-heirs with Christ to the crown of glory (Romans 8:17). One of the ways we can know that we are meeting and overcoming our crosses, living in at-one-ment, is when we can *joyfully* face each difficult problem.

Instead of dwelling on our own crosses, let's concentrate on helping others with theirs. As we follow Christ's example of loving service, He leads us to fulfillment. The door is open; we have virtue and understanding, and our faith is constantly renewed. We live in fellowship and oneness.

All the time, everywhere, we may show God's love to those around us. Eventually others will know, by the way we live and serve, that He walks with us. As we continue to follow the Way of the Cross, we will realize the crown of glory. What brings us the crown? *Faith-ful-ness!*

Individual Growth Experiences

1. Below is a cryptogram. Each letter of the sentence stands for another letter of the alphabet.
   Example:

   JESUS CHRIST
   TBKWK MAOQKN

   The letters in the example are not "keys" to the sentence on the next page.

72

Hint: Sentence structure helps here. What three-letter word begins many sentences? When you figure it out, you can fill in many of the other letters.

QWP KXENV EA MUAP UJ DUVP NWPV U KSV QXBMC MEGP SVL JPXGP EQWPXJ.

2. Below is a list of "causes." What "effects" or consequences could these "causes" set in motion? Take time to consider your responses. Some "causes" may have more than one possible "effect." Write your answers on a separate sheet of paper. There are no "right" or "wrong" answers. Remember that the law of karma must be met now or in another lifetime, or it can be fulfilled by living love (grace).

a. J makes fun of the way other people look.

b. B, offensive quarterback on his football team, tries to seriously injure M, a player on the other team who has dated B's girl.

c. No clerks are in sight. S finds it easy to put a pair of earrings, a necklace, and a bracelet or two in her purse. No one sees her, so she isn't caught.

d. Each night D's father drops his dimes into a coffee can on a closet shelf. D's allowance covers only necessities. His father probably won't notice it if D takes a few coins at a time. Now D takes the money he needs to experiment with "pot."

e. Two girls want to stay out past their family curfew times. Each tells her mother she is spending the night at the other's house. The two decide to drive around all night, snack at restaurants, talk, etc. Next day they are droopy, but no one is the wiser.

f. M is not only the wealthiest girl in school; she is also beautiful, a good student, and a cheerleader. A thinks she is snobbish and stand-offish, so she decides to show her a thing or two. A starts a gossip campaign, hinting that M has had an illegitimate child.

g. R has a good job in an office. He discovers that no one keeps a close check on the office supply closet. He takes paper, a stapler, transparent tape, etc., as he needs them for his own use.

3. Some ways to reach creative, loving attitudes through new ways of thinking and acting:
Read the following suggestions each day before you pray. Try to use them throughout the day as necessary.

a. Cross out guilt over past mistakes by knowing that God forgives us *as we forgive others*. (See Matthew 6:14, 15.)

b. Memorize the following quotation and use it each time there is a need to forgive someone: "Father, forgive them; they do not know what they are doing." (Luke 23:34, NEB)

c. Cross out personal negative karmic patterns by dwelling on the loving positive attitudes, instead of trying to battle the negative. Jesus told us to "resist not evil." (Matthew 5:39) The Bible says that we should overcome "evil" with good (Romans 12:21). Examples:

"I won't criticize others any more."	This can reinforce the problem because it is a negative statement.

Instead

"I will praise others and say uplifting things about them."	This is constructive reprogramming because it is a positive statement.

Here are examples of other positive affirmations:

"I am poised and confident in all I think and do, for I am God's child."

"I am patient with people and situations."

"I treat everyone as a part of myself, for I know that we are all one with each other and with God."

"Every person or experience teaches me something important. I learn the lesson and give thanks."

Group Activities

1. Using the situations described in #2 above, discuss several karmic consequences, "effects" that could develop from each one. Be sure to keep cases impersonal and positive, not judgmental or critical.

2. If people can change their selfish attitudes to loving ones, they can change their lives. With this idea in mind, explain how each of the effects discussed in #2 above could be overcome by love.

   Example: Part a. What might help J to be more kind? Perhaps to realize he is criticizing a part of himself, as well as a part of God, when he criticizes others, etc.

   Perhaps group members would like to act out or role-play some of the solutions. Remember: *Love* is the key.

3. See #3 above. After reading the parts of the exercise aloud in turn, formulate group and individual affirmations. Have each group member put his list on his bulletin board.

4. Groups of two might work the cryptogram in Individual Growth Experiences #1 together, or you can each work individually. Place the finished puzzle on your bulletin board if desired.

Cryptogram answer:

THE CROWN OF LIFE IS MINE WHEN I CAN TRULY LOVE AND SERVE OTHERS.

Lesson 11
THE LORD OUR GOD IS ONE

Bible Verse: ". . .for there is one God; and there is none other but he." (Mark 12:32, KJV)

Prayer Affirmation: Oh Lord, just as the body, mind, and soul are one, Your power, might and glory work as one in the earth. More and more, may I reflect Your oneness in my daily activities. (Based on Edgar Cayce reading 262-38.)

Introduction

Lord God, You are One;
Your oneness is complete.
Nothing can lessen You;
Nothing can increase You.
You are One, but not like
A number to be held or counted;
For number and change cannot affect You,
And You cannot be computed.
Your oneness encompasses all that is.

There is only one force, one mind, one presence—God. All that is in the cosmos is of God and is one with Him. His vibrations vary from the slow frequencies of visible matter to the rapid speed of invisible thought, existing in all his creations whether they be physical, mental, or spiritual. God lives in the moving atoms of all physical matter. He is as perfectly at work in the tiniest molecule as He is in the greatest planet. His power is at work in the receiving and sending of thought vibrations. He reveals Himself in varieties of spiritual or religious experiences. Yet, all of these expressions are aspects of the *one* God. The seeming differences exist only in our perception and understanding of how He works.

Outwardly, we can perceive His power, might, and glory in His creation:

"The heavens declare the glory of God,

the vault of heaven proclaims his handiwork;
day discourses of it to day,
night to night hands on the knowledge.

No utterance at all, no speech,
no sound that anyone can hear;
yet their voice goes out through all the earth,
and their message to the ends of the world."

(Psalms 19:1-4, JB)

Inwardly, we are aware of God through His Spirit. Jesus said, ". . .the kingdom of God is within you," and ". . .your Advocate, the Holy Spirit whom the Father will send in my name, will teach you everything. . ." (Luke 17:21, Lamsa; John 14:26, NEB)

All Creations Are One

God's Spirit lives in every thing and in everyone (Acts 17:28). All beings are one in Him. Because we are all one, our individual thoughts and actions, constructive or destructive, affect others (I Corinthians 12:26-27). Anything that happens to anyone anywhere—even on the other side of the world—affects us, too. All of the people on earth are one big family, connected in the oneness of God. When we really understand this, we know we must love everyone, for they are part of ourselves (I Corinthians 12:12-25).

Below is a diagram to help us understand our oneness with each other:

The Oneness of All Entities

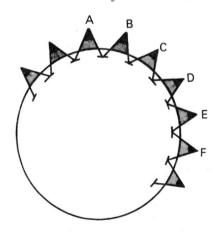

The circle represents the oneness of God's creation; the points represent a few of the myriad expressions of the oneness. At the conscious mind's level (darkened points), entities A, B, C, D, E, and F may perceive each other as separate beings. However, at the superconscious level (represented by the center of the circle) they are one, united with each other and all other entities. When they reach beyond the conscious and subconscious (dotted areas), they touch the superconscious (as in meditation), realizing their oneness with each other and with God.

Since God is all in all, it is impossible to be separated from His being.

"Where could I go to escape your spirit?
Where could I flee from your presence?
If I climb the heavens, you are there,
there too, if I lie in Sheol.[1]

If I flew to the point of sunrise
or westward across the sea,
your hand would still be guiding me,
your right hand holding me." (Psalms 139:7-10, JB)

Jesus said, ". . .The Lord our God, the Lord is one. . ." (Mark 12:29, RSV) He also stated, ". . .I am in my Father, and you in me and I in you." (John 14:20, NEB) This was His way of explaining oneness. He prayed to the Father that we, too, would become perfectly aware of our oneness with Him (John 17:20-23).

The Path to At-One-Ment

Jesus came to earth to show man the way to realize at-onement with God and man. Jesus learned to obey God's law through suffering, and realized oneness while in flesh. (See Hebrews 5:8-9.) Throughout His life He expressed His oneness with God in a practical and personal way. With words and actions in harmony with the law of love, He shared the oneness through healing, teaching, and helping those who were in need. He revealed to men their true natures: He said, ". . .Ye are gods. . ."[2] He loved men so much that He even entered death to show them the way to *life* (John 10:10).

Jesus' help for mankind did not end with His crucifixion and

---

1. *Sheol* means the realm of death. Some Bible versions translate the word as "hell."
2. John 10:34, KJV; Psalms 82:6, KJV. The word "gods" is the Hebrew *elohiym*, and is the same plural word used throughout the Old Testament (among others) to refer to God. It is the same word used in Genesis 1:1, "In the beginning God. . ." Although the word is the same, translators alternately render it "God" or "gods," depending on the context in which it is used. "Ye are gods," then, could be translated, "Ye are God."

death. *He still lives*—His guidance still continues. Even now He helps us; all we have to do is be willing to receive His help. He is bringing all men to the realization of at-one-ment. He said, "And I shall draw all men to myself, when I am lifted up from the earth." (John 12:32, NEB)

Tuning In to At-One-Ment

All over the world radio stations are broadcasting their programs. Whether or not we hear them depends on choice. We choose whether to tune them in or not. We might compare God to the radio stations, with Christ as His transmitter. His broadcast of abundance, love, healing, peace, joy, mercy, and kindness is constantly being beamed to everything and everyone. He never stops His "broadcast" of love. Yet, we can choose to listen or to tune Him out.

How do we tune in to station G-O-D? We follow the path of the Christ: We believe that God is, seek to harmonize our wills with His, center our Ideal in Him, pray and meditate, give up our selfishness through living love, and serve others. As we start to do these things the best we can, sooner or later we tune in to oneness.

People experience attunement to the oneness in many ways.[3] Some have exciting or dramatic religious experiences. There are those who actually hear the voice of God's loving guidance. Many experience God's advice as a "feeling" of what they need to do. Some "see" pictures that help them in the present, tell them of things to come, or explain things that have happened in the past. Others may not see or hear God's guidance but they feel a profound love and peace through their relationship of faith in Him. Still others don't seem to experience anything when they pray and meditate, but they discover that bit by bit their lives change for the better.

We don't have to have a great religious or psychic experience to become aware of God's guidance. As we seek Him and follow our Ideal the best we can, our meditations, thoughts, and activities grow more and more in harmony with Him and we become less selfish and more loving. As we live love, the habits of our lower natures are overcome. Our lives are filled with peace and joy as we become aware of our oneness with God, everyone, and everything.

---

3. The gifts of the spirit may be described as telepathy, intuition, precognition, clairvoyance, psychokinesis, dream interpretation, healing, etc. The Bible describes these gifts in other terms, in 1 Corinthians 12:5-11.

Conclusion

God is active in every plane, in every force, and in every level of our being—physical, mental, and spiritual. Only our selfish wills can keep Him from expressing His perfection through us. Spiritual understanding is not far away—it is within us. We can tune in to it as we live loving unselfishness. As we let go of our selfish natures and let God work through us, we begin to have harmony at all the levels of our being. Physically, the atoms of our bodies vibrate in health and strength. Mentally, our thoughts are creative, stimulating, uplifting, and peaceful. We are united to our spiritual Ideal and it leads us to complete attunement with His oneness, His loving grace.

The more we experience the oneness, the more we realize that every creation of God has a special purpose in His plan. Animals, plants, rocks, and even grains of sand all have their purposes. Every individual soul has a purpose, too. The kind parent giving water to a sick child, a skilled physician helping the ill, and the spiritual healer using a touch of love to open blind eyes are each serving their purposes in their own ways. They are expressing God's oneness with their individual talents. Our talents may be very different, and seemingly very simple, but we can serve in our own ways to fulfill our purposes in God's plan. As we bring our desires, hearts, minds, and souls into harmony with God's love, we find the oneness and our purpose in it. Also, we are able to help others discover that,

> ". . .God is one and beside him there is no
> other. And to love him with all your heart,
> all your understanding, all your strength,
> and to love your neighbor as yourself—that
> is far more than any burnt offerings or
> sacrifices." (Mark 12:32-33, NEB)

Individual Growth Experiences

1. Choose a word or phrase that describes God and His oneness. Create a design from your "God-Words." Examples:

2. The Bean Game
   Take two small plastic bags and fifteen dried beans in each.
   Put a "+" on the front of one bag and a "-" on the outside of
   the other bag. For one week or more, play the "Bean Game"
   with yourself. Every time you say a negative or critical
   remark, transfer a bean from the "+" bag to the "-" bag. When
   you say something constructive or positive, move a bean from
   the "-" to the "+" bag. At the end of each day count how many
   beans you have in each bag. You know your true spiritual self
   is winning when you have more beans in the "+" bag at the end
   of the day. Your spiritual self wins when you reach the day
   that you can transfer all your "-" beans to the "+" bag.

Study Group Activities

1. Do #1 above as a group activity. Share designs. Take them
   home and place them on bulletin boards.
2. Do #2 above as a group game. Let each member make and fill
   his own plastic bags with beans at home, or do it as a group
   endeavor with the members making the bags at the end of a
   meeting. After a week of moving the beans back and forth
   daily, let the members share their insights with the group.
   Emphasize the positive insights and experiences.

Lesson 12
LOVE

Bible Verse: ". . .there are three things that last for ever: faith, hope, and love; but the greatest of them all is love." (I Corinthians 13:13, NEB)

Prayer Affirmation: Father, through the love that You have shown in the world in Your Son, the Christ, make us more aware that You are love. (Based on Edgar Cayce reading 262-43; see also I John 4:16.)

Introduction

God is Love; Love is God (I John 4:8). Love expressing Itself is life, the Creative Force in action. Divine love is everywhere and in everything, for each of God's creations is, at the core of its being, a complete expression of His love. The law of the cosmos is love, and all laws—including the law of faith, the law of karma, and the law of the forces of the earth—are based on it. When we willingly live love, we fulfill all of God's laws, perfect our lives, and realize and express the eternal oneness (Romans 13:10; Matthew 5:17-20).

The Importance of Love

When Love created everything, It looked upon it, saw that it was good, and blessed it (Genesis 1:31). When we begin to touch at-one-ment's love, we see good in everyone and everything (Titus 1:15). When we see the truth, the good, in all, we bring love's healing, cleansing, and blessings to everything we touch, including the mineral, plant, and animal kingdoms.

Love is extremely important to everyone. Some children are stunted and can die if they do not receive love. People of all ages can become weak or ill if they feel unloved. If anxious people begin to give and receive love, they are able to overcome feelings of depression and inadequacy, realize a new self-respect, and lead more productive lives.

Since Love is God, Love is our supply. Love fulfills all our needs. Do we lack anything? If we do, let's ask ourselves, "Where are we not applying love?" God *never* withholds blessings from His children. However, *our* unloving attitudes can keep us from experiencing His presence and receiving the full supply of His abundance. Our supply and success can be blocked if we are selfish and don't fully express God's love in our lives.

God is our Creator, but we are co-workers with Him, and we affect His creation and our lives with our minds and wills. Since He is Love, our lives overflow with harmony and beauty when we cooperate with His plan. If we are experiencing difficulties, we need to realize that they are self-created. Each problem is an opportunity for us to look within and learn a lesson in unselfishness. Realizing this, we can inspect the attitudes behind our problems and transform them through the power of love.

In the midst of difficulties we can count our blessings and see God's love in all situations and in all people. Or we can dwell on their negative aspects and become overwhelmed by them. If we refuse to learn the lessons presented by our problems and continue to misuse our creative power for our own selfish purposes, we can hurt others, crush ideals, cause revolts, and even wreck civilizations. How much more wonderful it is to use the power of love to help, encourage, uplift, and bring peace and blessings to the world and its people! Which will we choose? Will we choose selfishness, or the way of the Christ?

The Perfect Expression of Love

The dynamic power of love brought Christ Jesus to the earth to create a way for men to realize oneness with their Creator and express it. Christ's love for mankind was so great that the Father allowed Him to enter the earth to lead men to the realization that they are eternal beings. (See John 3:16.)

Jesus Christ perfectly expressed the Father's love. He told us that as God's children we too can express love perfectly. (See Matthew 5:48.) We show His love when we do whatever needs to be done, without selfish motives, expecting nothing in return. We express love when we do the best we can with the talents we have, however small they may seem to be. We live love when we encourage or help others. When we truly love, we completely forget about ourselves. Then our love is so powerful that we are even willing to give our lives for other people (John 15:13; Matthew 10:39). How can we live such perfect love? By letting

God live through us. United with His consciousness, we live the love that is beyond the world's understanding.

The Test of Love

The golden thread of the Father's love is woven throughout all divinely inspired Scriptures. The Bible says, "There is no room for fear in love; perfect love banishes fear. For fear brings with it the pains of judgment, and anyone who is afraid has not attained to love in its perfection. We love because he loved us first. But if a man says, 'I love God,' while hating his brother, he is a liar. If he does not love the brother whom he has seen, it cannot be that he loves God whom he has not seen. And indeed this command comes to us from Christ himself: that he who loves God must also love his brother." (I John 4:18-21, NEB)

The Apostle Paul wrote, ". . .I am convinced that there is nothing in death or life, in the realm of spirits or super-human powers, in the world as it is or the world as it shall be, in the forces of the universe, in heights or depths—nothing in all creation that can separate us from the love of God in Christ Jesus our Lord." (Romans 8:38, NEB) The Apostle John summed up the revelation of God's love: "God loved the world so much that he gave his only Son, that everyone who has faith in him may not die but have eternal life." (John 3:16, NEB)

Jesus, the Master, emphasized the importance of love: "This is my commandment, that ye love one another, as I have loved you." (See John 13:34.) "There is no greater love than this, when a man lays down his life for the sake of his friends." (John 15:13, Lamsa) He also said, "Love your enemies, and pray for those who persecute you. . .For if you love only those who love you, what credit is that to you?" (Matthew 5:44, 46, PB) Fulfilling the law of love, then, means loving everyone, not just those who love us. If we love only those who love us, we haven't the slightest idea of what divine love is. We haven't even begun to develop until we love our enemies—those who oppose our egos. If we allow slights, slurs, suspicions, etc., to affect us, we aren't fully experiencing love.

When we really love perfectly, we are freed from saying unkind words, or being disappointed in things, people, and conditions. When we truly love, we recognize God's essence in everyone and everything. When we really live Jesus' commandment of love, we will be aware that Christ lives in us as He lives in the Father, and that all of us are one. (See John 14.)

84

Love Is Giving

When we love, we give without asking anything in return. We think of others' needs before our own. We see some good in everyone. This is the kind of love that Jesus showed us in His life, death, and resurrection. He loves all of us so much that He said, ". . .be assured, I am with you always, to the end of time." (Matthew 28:20, NEB) He gives us the sympathy, comfort, and strength we need to meet every situation in life; all we have to do is receive them.

Jesus perfectly expressed not only love, but all the soul qualities mentioned in this book. In living the way, He became the way—our perfect pattern for living. As we follow His teachings, our loving thoughts and actions will share His light with those in darkness. We never need to feel that we have wasted our efforts when we unselfishly help our families, friends, or others. The loving service that we give is an expression of His Holy Spirit and can never be lost, for love cannot die; it is eternal. Unselfish service is actually built into our souls and into the soul-memories of those we aid. It lights their lives and continues to bless them, to be shared with still more people, and even to help future generations. What peace there will be on earth when we understand the depth of Christ's love and live it ourselves!

Living Love

God never intended for man's awareness to be separated from His. God, the First Cause, created the world as an expression of His love, not as a place for man's entrapment. He gave man the ability to know always his oneness with Him. Even when we had cut off our awareness of Him through selfishness, God showed the extent of His great love by sending His beloved Son to show us the way to find Him again. When we live perfectly the Christ's pattern of love, we fulfill karmic law and overcome the material plane, death, and the need for further incarnations (Matthew 5:48; Romans 13:10). We are freed to experience the limitless oneness of God and His creation.

The Bible describes love this way:

> "I may speak in tongues of men or of angels, but if I am without love, I am a sounding gong or a clanging cymbal. I may have the gift of prophecy and know every hidden truth; I may have faith strong enough to move mountains; but if I have no love, I am nothing. I may dole out all I possess, or even give my body to be

burnt, but if I have no love, I am none the better.

"Love is patient; love is kind and envies no one. Love is never boastful, nor conceited, nor rude; never selfish, not quick to take offence. Love keeps no score of wrongs; does not gloat over other men's sins, but delights in the truth. There is nothing love cannot face; there is no limit to its faith, its hope, and its endurance.

"Love will never come to an end. Are there prophets? Their work will be over. Are there tongues of ecstasy? They will cease. Is there knowledge? It will vanish away; for our knowledge and our prophecy alike are partial, and the partial vanishes when wholeness comes. When I was a child, my speech, my outlook, and my thoughts were all childish. When I grew up, I had finished with childish things. Now we see only puzzling reflections in a mirror, but then we shall see face to face. My knowledge now is partial; then it will be whole, like God's knowledge of me. In a word, there are three things that last forever: faith, hope, and love; but the greatest of them all is love."

(I Corinthians 13, NEB)

Individual Growth Experiences

1. Choose a favorite Bible verse that uses the word "love." First, memorize it. Then write it in your own words. How can you apply it in your life?

2. Make a "self-portrait." Look back at the work you have placed on your bulletin board or have saved from study group sessions. Choose pictures, poetry, symbols, affirmations, prayers, handwork, etc., that you feel really represent you. If you feel that you need more items, use magazines, newspapers, cards, photos, or any other materials that help complete the "real you." Pray about the project.

   Now create a collage or a simple design or drawing based on the items you have chosen. You may use construction paper, felt, a poster board, or whatever else you may like for the background of your self-portrait. You may wish to use watercolors, paints, crayons, chalks, felt-tipped pens, or sewing materials to complete your self-study. Remember your Ideal as you work. When the self-portrait is complete, frame or mount it and hang it in your room to remind you of your Ideal. Your work may present you with many interesting insights as time goes by. Don't consider your self-portrait an unchangeable thing. You may receive inspiration from time to time that may cause you to want to change it.

Study Group Activities

1. Do #1 above. Let the group discuss and compare their efforts.
2. Do #2 above. You may need magazines, scissors, rubber cement, etc. Let each person share his self-portrait and the insights he gained from making it. What symbols did he choose? Why? Remind the group to look at their bulletin boards for ideas.
3. Candlelight Prayer Service (Read through this activity before doing it.)

   The group will need enough white votive (small, fat) candles for each member. They will also need a large white candle and a heat-proof glass or metal flat-bottomed pan.

   Put about two inches of salt or sand in the bottom of the pan. Place the large candle on a stand and put it next to the pan. (Be sure to use a sturdy table to hold all the materials.) Now set the small candles on the table near the large one. Darken the room if possible.

   Let the large candle stand for God. The smaller candles can stand for each person as a light in Him. When the group is quiet, light the large candle.

   Each person should prayerfully approach the table, pick up a candle, and say a one-sentence prayer, aloud or silently. Then he should light his candle from the big one and stand the smaller one in the pan. After all the members have had their turns, let them form a circle, join hands, and have a moment of prayerful silence, experiencing a unity of love with one another and with God. (It is a good idea to extinguish the candles before meditation.)

SYMBOLS CHART

All communication, verbal and written, involves symbols. Notes symbolize musical sounds; letters are symbols for speech sounds; words are symbols for ideas. Symbolic meanings change with usage and the passage of time.

Traditional meanings for the basic symbols below may be interpreted in many ways. The chart should prove helpful, however, in unlocking hidden meanings behind current symbols. It should also help the seeker invent symbols to convey his own meanings and ideas.

Circle: God, eternity, superconscious, sun, masculine or positive pole (+).

Half-moon: Subconscious, moon, receptivity, feminine or negative pole (-).

Vertical line: Conscious mind reaching up (seeking God); divine mind reaching down; man lowering his awareness into the physical plane.

Horizontal line: Man in the earth, exploring materiality.

Dot in circle: God, or an individual soul dwelling in the circle of God's love.

Yang-Yin: Oriental symbol for the positive (+) and negative (-) polarities in perfect balance—God.

Circle divided by cross: The four earth elements (fire, air, earth, water) within the circle of God; earth.

Two circles side by side: Eternity.

Square: Another symbol for earth; balanced life.

Triangle, point up: Fire; balance of mind, body, and spirit reaching toward God.

Triangle, point down: Water; the Holy Trinity (Father, Son, Holy Spirit) reaching toward man.

Serpent: Lower meaning: kundalini force used to satisfy man's selfish desires. Higher meaning: wisdom; kundalini force united with God-Force selflessly.

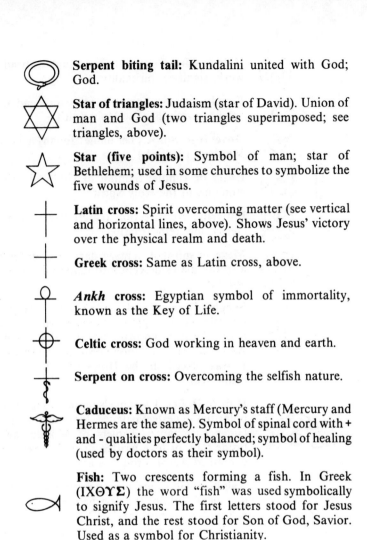

Serpent biting tail: Kundalini united with God; God.

Star of triangles: Judaism (star of David). Union of man and God (two triangles superimposed; see triangles, above).

Star (five points): Symbol of man; star of Bethlehem; used in some churches to symbolize the five wounds of Jesus.

Latin cross: Spirit overcoming matter (see vertical and horizontal lines, above). Shows Jesus' victory over the physical realm and death.

Greek cross: Same as Latin cross, above.

***Ankh* cross:** Egyptian symbol of immortality, known as the Key of Life.

Celtic cross: God working in heaven and earth.

Serpent on cross: Overcoming the selfish nature.

Caduceus: Known as Mercury's staff (Mercury and Hermes are the same). Symbol of spinal cord with + and - qualities perfectly balanced; symbol of healing (used by doctors as their symbol).

Fish: Two crescents forming a fish. In Greek (ΙΧΘΥΣ) the word "fish" was used symbolically to signify Jesus. The first letters stood for Jesus Christ, and the rest stood for Son of God, Savior. Used as a symbol for Christianity.

Trinity symbols: Triangle   Three fish   Clover Fleur-de-lis

Crown: Symbol of the kingship of Christ; the "crown of life"; perfect purity; overcoming the lower nature, including sin, death and the grave.

Crown of thorns: Symbol of suffering, particularly Jesus' suffering and sacrifice.

Halo or aura: Circle of light around the head; in art work, signifies spirituality.

 Fire: In art, sometimes placed on forehead or top of head to symbolize the Holy Spirit.

 Dove: Holy Spirit. (The name "Jonah" means dove. Matthew 12:39-41.)

  Lamp or candle: Symbol of God's illumination; guidance of the Holy Spirit.

 Butterfly: Resurrection (caterpillar to butterfly); eternal life; reincarnation.

 Maze, or spiral: As a maze: darkness, confusion. As a spiral: man's descent into materiality or upward growth.

 Shepherd's crook and Aaron's rod: God's guidance (as reflected through the seven *chakras* or centers in man). Jesus is known as "the Good Shepherd." Aaron carried the almond branch for Moses to use. It was placed in the Holy of Holies. (See also *caduceus.*)

 Holy of Holies: Two angels representing the + and - polarities in perfect balance. Jar of manna stood for God's sustenance. Tablets of Mosaic law were inside (law of love written in one's heart). It also contained Aaron's rod (see above).

 Rainbow: God's promise to restore mankind to at-one-ment without the destruction of the world by water. (See Genesis 9:8-16.) The seven colors of the rainbow are symbolized in man in the *chakras* and reflected in the endocrine system. The colors whirling in perfect harmony combine as the white light. (See color chart.)

 Menorah: Same as the rainbow. Symbol of each light *(chakra)* in perfect balance. The Jewish candlestick. Also represents the six days of creation and the seventh day of rest.

COLOR SYMBOLISM

Color	Higher Meaning	Lower Meaning
Purple or violet	Humility; God-centeredness instead of self-centeredness; service.	Dirty purple—pride; vanity.
Blue (includes indigo)	Spirituality; loyalty; listening for and following God's guidance; truth; faith; spiritual activity.	Dirty blue—depression; lack of faith.
Green	Growth; nature; healing.	Dirty green—envy.
Yellow	Sun; energy; happiness; mental activity.	Dirty yellow—fear; cowardice.
Orange	Self-control; thoughtfulness.	Dirty orange—laziness.
Red	Life force; energy; physical activity.	Dirty red—hate; anger; lust.
White	Perfect balance and harmony of all colors; purity; holiness; light.	
Gray	In art, humility is sometimes symbolized by gray (the color of ashes).	Illness; sadness.
Black		Death; darkness; sin; ignorance; confusion.
Gold	Metallic gold color signifies purity of actions; divinity; nobility. (Gold is a product that is refined and the impurities are removed from it.)	

BIBLIOGRAPHY

Allen, Eula. *The Creation Trilogy.* Virginia Beach, Va.: A.R.E. Press, 1974.

Economic Healing. Virginia Beach, Va.: A.R.E. Press, 1970.

Holy Bible, Authorized King James Version. Cleveland and New York: The World Publishing Company.

Jerusalem Bible, The. Garden City, New York: Doubleday and Company, Inc., 1968.

Lamsa, George M. *The New Testament,* Philadelphia: A.J. Holman Company, 1968.

New Catholic Edition of the Holy Bible. New York: Catholic Publishing Company, 1957.

New English Bible, The. New York: Oxford University Press, 1971.

New Testament in Modern English, The. J.B. Phillips, trans. New York: The Macmillan Company, 1958.

Original Readings on *A Search for God,* Book I. Virginia Beach, Va.: A.R.E. Press.

Prayer Group Readings, The. Virginia Beach, Va.: A.R.E. Press, 1971.

Revised Standard Version of the Holy Bible. New York: Thomas Nelson and Sons, 1946 and 1952.

Shelley, Violet M. *Symbols and the Self.* Virginia Beach, Va.: A.R.E. Press, 1965.

Strong, James. *Strong's Exhaustive Concordance of the Bible.* New York: Abingdon Press, 1890.

Sugrue, Thomas. *There Is a River.* New York: Dell Publishing Company, Inc., 1969.

Torah, The. Philadelphia: The Jewish Publication Society of America, 1962.

Wilson, Frank E. *An Outline of Christian Symbolism.* New York: Morehouse-Barlow Co., 1961.

RECOMMENDED SUPPLEMENTARY READING

Listed below are A.R.E. publications which may be of aid for study. A price list may be obtained by writing A.R.E. Press, P.O. Box 595, Virginia Beach, VA 23451.

The Handbook for A.R.E. Study Groups
Edgar Cayce and Group Dynamics
Meditation—Gateway to Light
Meditation and the Mind of Man
A Dictionary—Definitions and Comments from the Edgar Cayce Readings
Dreams, the Language of the Unconscious
Dreams—Your Magic Mirror
Symbols and the Self
God's Other Door (concerning life after death)
There Is a River
Many Mansions
The Creation Trilogy (includes the following three books, which can also be ordered separately:)
Before the Beginning
The River of Time
You Are Forever

THE EDGAR CAYCE LEGACIES

Among the vast resources which have grown out of the late Edgar Cayce's work are:

The Readings: Available for examination and study at the Association for Research and Enlightenment, Inc.,(A.R.E.®) at Virginia Beach, Va., are 14,256 readings consisting of 49,135 pages of verbatim psychic material plus related correspondence. The readings are the clairvoyant discourses given by Cayce while he was in a self-induced hypnotic sleep-state. These discourses were recorded in shorthand and then typed. Copious indexing and cross-indexing make the readings readily accessible for study.

Research and Information: Medical information which flowed through Cayce is being researched and applied by the research divisions of the Edgar Cayce Foundation. Work is also being done with dreams and other aspects of ESP. Much information is disseminated through the A.R.E. Press publications, *A.R.E. News* and *The A.R.E. Journal.* Coordination of a nationwide program of lectures and conferences is in the hands of the Department of Education. A library specializing in psychic literature is available to the public with books on loan to members. An extensive tape library has A.R.E. lectures available for purchase. Resource material has been made available for authors, resulting in the publication of scores of books, booklets and other material.

A.R.E. Study Groups: The Edgar Cayce material is most valuable when worked with in an A.R.E. Study Group, the text for which is *A Search for God,* Books I and II. These books are the outcome of eleven years of work by Edgar Cayce with the first A.R.E. group and represent the distillation of wisdom which flowed through him in the trance condition. Hundreds of A.R.E. groups flourish throughout the United States and other countries. Their primary purpose is to assist the members to know their relationship to their Creator and to become channels of love and service to others. The groups are nondenominational and avoid ritual and dogma. There are no dues or fees required to join a group although contributions may be accepted.

Membership: A.R.E. has an open-membership policy which offers attractive benefits.

For more information write A.R.E., Box 595, Virginia Beach, Va. 23451. To obtain information about publications, please direct your query to A.R.E. Press. To obtain information about joining or perhaps starting an A.R.E. Study Group, please direct your letter to the Study Group Department.